THE COMPLETE GUIDE TO BOXER DOGS

Ruth Shirk and Erin Hotovy

LP Media Inc. Publishing

Text copyright © 2020 by LP Media Inc.

www.lpmedia.org

Publication Data

Ruth Shirk and Erin Hotovy

The Complete Guide to Boxer Dogs ---- First edition.

Summary: "Successfully raising a Boxer Dog from puppy to old age" --- Provided by publisher.

ISBN: 978-1-952069-72-7

[1.Boxer Dogs --- Non-Fiction] I. Title.

Design by Sorin Rădulescu

First hardcover edition, 2020

Cover Photo Courtesy of Marcus D. Sarazin - www.MarcusDPhotography.com

TABLE OF CONTENTS

CHAPTER 1
Boxer History **8**
The Charismatic Boxer **9**
The History of the Boxer **11**
Is a Boxer the Right Fit for You? **12**

CHAPTER 2
Choosing a Boxer **14**
Buying vs. Adopting **14**
How to Find a Reputable Breeder **16**
Researching Breeders **18**
Health Tests and Certifications **19**
Breeder Contracts and Guarantees **21**
Choosing the Perfect Pup **22**

CHAPTER 3
Preparing Your Home for Your Boxer **24**
Preparing Your Humans **24**
Preparing Your Pets **27**
Giving the Boxer Indoor Space **29**
Getting Your Yard Ready for Your Boxer **31**
Necessary Supplies for Your Boxer **33**

CHAPTER 4
Bringing Your Boxer Home **34**
The Importance of Having a Plan **34**
The Ride Home **35**
The First Night Home **35**

Keeping Your Boxer Comfortable at the Vet **38**
Educating Your Boxer **40**
Cost Breakdown for the First Year **41**

CHAPTER 5
Being a Puppy Parent **42**
Setting Realistic Expectations **43**
Many Noises **43**
Common Puppy Problems **45**
Separation Anxiety **47**

CHAPTER 6
Potty Training **50**
Options for Potty Training **51**
Keeping it Positive **53**
Playpens and Doggy Doors **55**

CHAPTER 7
Socializing with People and Animals **56**
Greeting New Human Friends **57**
Interacting with Other Animals **60**
Introducing Your Boxer to Pet Friends **61**
Pack Mentality **64**
Raising Multiple Boxers **65**
Boxers Who Hate Other Pets **66**

CHAPTER 8
Physical and Mental Exercise **68**
Exercise Requirements **69**
Physical Exercise **71**
Keeping the Boxer's Mind Alert **73**
Occupying Your Boxer When You are Busy **74**

CHAPTER 9
Training Your Boxer **76**
Setting Clear Expectations **77**
Skinner Was Right: Using Operant Conditioning . . . **78**
The Best Reinforcements **78**
Stay Positive **81**
Hiring a Trainer **83**
Are You Doing it Right? **84**

CHAPTER 10

Basic Commands **86**

Sit **87**

Lie Down **87**

Stay **87**

Come **88**

Off **89**

Drop **89**

Walk **90**

Advanced Commands **92**

Shake/High Five **92**

Crawl **92**

Sit Pretty **92**

Spin **93**

CHAPTER 11

Traveling With Your Boxer **94**

Dog Carriers and Car Restraints **94**

Preparing Your Dog for Car Rides **97**

Flying and Hotel Stays **97**

Kenneling vs. Dog Sitters **98**

Tips and Tricks for Traveling **100**

CHAPTER 12

Nutrition **102**

Importance of Good Diet **103**

The Role of Protein in Your Boxer's Diet **104**

Wet Vs. Dry Dog Food **105**

Cooking for Your Boxer **107**

Feeding Table Scraps **107**

Treats **109**

Weight Management **110**

CHAPTER 13

Grooming Your Boxer **112**

Coat Basics **112**

Bath Time **112**

Time for a Pedicure **113**

Brushing Teeth **114**

Cleaning Ears and Eyes **115**

CHAPTER 14

Basic Health Care **116**

Fleas and Ticks **117**

Worms and Internal Parasites **119**

Natural Health Care and Your Boxer **121**

Vaccinations **121**

Pet Insurance **122**

CHAPTER 15

Advanced Boxer Health and Your Aging Boxer **124**

Boxer First Aid Basics **125**

Genetic Health of Boxers **127**

Illness and Injury Prevention **128**

Caring For Your Aging Boxer **129**

When it's Time to Say Goodbye **131**

CHAPTER 1
Boxer History

Boxers are one of the most popular dog breeds in America. As long as they are properly trained, they are a delight to be around. If you do not properly socialize them, however, you will be the one that ends up being trained. Following the advice in this book will help you understand boxers before you bring one home, because the breed is not for everyone. Yet, if it is right for you, then you will have a very loyal companion who loves to have fun.

Photo Courtesy of Jennifer Bentley

The Charismatic Boxer

When you first meet a boxer, you will see a very intelligent dog. Gaze deep into a boxer's eyes, and you can tell that there is a lot going on inside his brain. You need to be prepared to harness their intelligence to work with you. Otherwise, they can be very destructive. Their high energy level often leads them to try antics that will leave you shaking your head.

Photo Courtesy of Nicole Monan

You will need to learn to do all your activities with your boxer at your side. In fact, getting your boxer to not lay on your feet when you sit down or give you enough room to sit comfortably on the couch may be one of the biggest struggles you face on a daily basis. Forget doing anything on the floor unless it is a boxer-friendly activity.

Boxers do well in busy families where life centers around the home. They suffer incredible separation anxiety, so expect them to want to be in on all the action, whether it is a game of football in the backyard or baking cookies in the kitchen. While your boxer may not eat your child's homework, if your son or daughter chooses to work while sprawled on the floor, don't be surprised if you end up having to write a note to the child's teacher explaining why there is a big muddy paw print in the middle of it.

FUN FACT
Breed Popularity

The Boxer is the 10th most popular dog breed in the United States, according to the American Kennel Club (AKC).

*Photo Courtesy of
Laurie Roberson
Topline Boxers*

The History of the Boxer

The very first boxer was bred in Germany. This dog breed was one of the first to be seriously developed by the Germans. Ancestors of this breed, however, were known as early as 2000 B.C., when they were developed by the Assyrian Army for their great strength and loyalty. These Assyrian dogs, called Bullenbeissers, were bred to hold

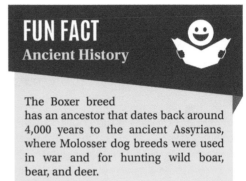

FUN FACT
Ancient History

The Boxer breed has an ancestor that dates back around 4,000 years to the ancient Assyrians, where Molosser dog breeds were used in war and for hunting wild boar, bear, and deer.

down large animals, like wild boars, until they could be killed by hunters. The dogs were then imported into Europe and other places where they formed the foundation for many breeds including bulldogs. While the Bullenbeisser is an extinct breed now, its great courage is still very evident in the breed today.

Stand back from your boxer and you can still see some of the original breed characteristics of the Bullenbeisser in the breed today, as they were short haired dogs with large heads and powerful muzzles. Their upper lips drooped, and their legs were very quick. All recorded Bullenbeissers were fawn or brindle in color.

About 1830, wealthy landowners introduced European dogs resembling bulldogs to Germany. This resulted in white marking being introduced to the Bullenbeisser breed along with the dog getting a little shorter.

The first standard for the boxer was written in 1895, and even over 100 years later, it remains the standard for the breed. About the same time, the first boxer entered the show arena; a little bitch named Alt's Flora. The first Breedbook was created in 1905 with Muhlbauer's Flocki listed as the first entry. Her mom was Alt's Flora and her dad was a white English bulldog named Dr. Tonessen's Tom.

All boxers in America can trace their heritage back to four dogs that were bred in Germany. The first to enter the United States was Sigurd von Dom. While the dog was imported by Charles Ludwig, he was soon sold to Barmere Kennels, who spent the next several years showing him across the United States introducing many people to this loyal breed.

The second dog to enter America was Dorian von Marienhof. He was widely shown in the United States and in England where he won the working group at the Westminster Dog Show in 1937. He went on to sire 40 champions. The remaining two dogs that were instrumental in introducing this breed to America were Lustig von Dom and Utz von Dom.

11

Is a Boxer the Right Fit for You?

A Boxer may be the right breed for you if you are looking for an active dog who loves to be in on everything that you are doing. If you want a quiet dog who does not shed or drool, then do not get a Boxer. If you ignore this advice, you can expect to be covered in dog drool every day and to be given wet slobbery kisses. This breed may require you to clean your home more frequently, but the love they give in return is worth it for many Boxer owners.

Make sure to consider that this dog needs at least 40 minutes of exercise every day. It can come in a variety of ways including dog weight pulling, agility training, or long runs. If you choose to ignore this fact, the Boxer will remind you by becoming hyperactive and destructive. If you are not able to take your dog on walks or spend time playing in the backyard, this breed may be difficult to care for.

This dog's background as a protector can be a problem if you do not take the time to socialize the dog properly when it is young. The older the dog is, the more difficult the task becomes. You may want to enroll your dog in a puppy class shortly after bringing him home. At the same time, Boxers are eager to please. This trait makes them an ideal candidate for Good Citizenship Certificates. It is important that you are willing to spend time and money on training classes. Untrained and unsocialized Boxers may cause problems in your household because they are so difficult to control.

Photo Courtesy of
Theresa Mitchell

Photo Courtesy of
Joelle Bezanson

Boxers do well in big families where something is constantly happening. They are great with children as long as they are introduced properly. While this breed is generally happiest in a large family home, they also do well in apartments and other tight quarters as long as they get enough mental and physical exercise. Otherwise, they can become very destructive. This dog is not a good fit for someone who spends a lot of time outside of the home and plans on leaving their dog alone for long periods of time. This breed will quickly become unhappy if they do not receive adequate attention. Be realistic about the amount of time that you have to give to a dog before you agree to take a Boxer into your home.

Unfortunately, some apartment complexes and mobile home parks have restrictions against Boxers as they group them with other aggressive breed dogs. While most Boxers are not aggressive, unless you count licking you to death with kisses, the restrictions remain. A few home insurance companies have the same restrictions, so prior to acquiring a Boxer; make sure you look at your home insurance policy to ensure that you are covered.

If you still feel a Boxer is the dog you want, then the rest of this book is for you. We will discuss how to choose the right Boxer and proper training techniques. Be sure that you are not part of the problem before you blame bad behavior on the loving Boxer breed.

CHAPTER 2
Choosing a Boxer

Once you have made the decision to get a Boxer, then the next question becomes where to get one. There are great Boxers available at many animal shelters, but you should also consider whether buying a Boxer from a reputable breeder is the right choice for you.

Buying vs. Adopting

While it is possible to find young pups at rescue facilities, the dogs at rescue facilities are more commonly adults. While that allows you to skip the puppy stage of chewing on everything, it also means that you often end up with a dog who was placed at a rescue facility because he had behavior issues. On the other hand, the dog may have ended up there simply because the previous owners did not have time to train him.

There are advantages to getting a Boxer from a rescue facility. You are often saving two lives when you adopt a dog. You are saving the life of the animal you are adopting, and you are opening space so that another dog can be rescued. Different rescue groups and shelters have different adoption requirements. Secure a copy of the requirements so that you can make sure that you meet all of them. If you have owned a pet in the past, do

Photo Courtesy of
Marcus D. Sarazin
www.MarcusDPhotography.com

not be surprised if you are asked to provide a pet statement. It may seem invasive for a shelter or rescue organization to ask you questions about your house, your time commitments, or the people in your household, but screening potential owners has a purpose. Shelters want to ensure that their dogs only need to be re-homed once and that the dog will have everything he needs to be happy and healthy. If you find that your current situation does not fit the adoption requirements, talk with an adoption specialist about things you can change to have a dog-friendly home and lifestyle.

"Definitely take some time or several trips to the rescue to see and visit with a boxer you might be interested in. Watch for signs of aggression. Many boxers get re homed or given up because their owners are not equipped or lack the time needed to invest in the boxer to train them. Boxers are energetic, rambunctious dogs! That is what makes them so fun, but all that energy needs to be harnessed and trained or you will have a high strung boxer with no manners! Find out as much about the history of the boxer you are interested in that you can. Are they able to be with other dogs; male or female, are they good around kids, other pets like cats, do they have anxiety issues when left alone. The more questions you ask the better!"

Brad & Gail Quistorff
Breezy Boxers

Some Boxers end up in foster care. Most fosterers are dog-loving people who have the experience to correct some poor behaviors. This can be a great advantage if you are lucky enough to find one, as it can be like sending your Boxer to a private trainer for a while. Instead of living in a shelter with a lot of other animals, foster dogs live in a person's home. Foster situations vary, but oftentimes foster homes include children and other pets, which allows foster dogs to socialize. If you adopt a Boxer from a foster home, you'll have the opportunity to speak with the fosterer about the dog's unique behavioral traits or past experiences.

Boxers who come from rescues are often less expensive than buying from a breeder. Usually, rescues will not ask more than $250 for an animal versus the $1,500 a breeder may want. Boxers adopted from shelters are usually fixed or you get a voucher to have them fixed. This can be an advantage if you are not looking to breed. Most have some basic health checkups done, but you get no guarantees. Most reputable breeders do offer health guarantees, and they only breed the very best animals.

Avoid puppy mills at all costs. These people are callous, and they breed indiscriminately and as often as possible. The quality of the Boxers coming out of a puppy mill is usually substantially less than from a reputable breeder. In fact, the quality is often less than you can find at your local shelter. If a "breeder" is breeding multiple dog breeds, does not know a lot about the breed, does not hold certifications for their dogs, or has generally shady business practices, they are likely running a puppy mill. You may be able to buy a "purebred" Boxer for a low price, but you'll later pay the price when your pup is unhealthy. Plus, buying from unethical breeders supports their business.

How to Find a Reputable Breeder

"You definitely want to purchase from a breeder that is transparent with you. If they are reluctant to show you the kenneling areas, or the parents, that is a huge red flag. What do they have to hide? Look for the classic boxer lines - do some research on the standard boxer. Too long of snouts, eyes too far apart, toes that are not in a firm knuckle position, chest that don't have that deep barrel, are some of the signs of bad breeding lines. Watch and meet the parents for personalities. Some personalities may not be inherited, where as some others can be. Ask about the health of the parents."

Brad & Gail Quistorff
Breezy Boxers

Photo Courtesy of
Nichole Edmonds

It can be difficult to find a reputable breeder. The first step is to make a list of possibilities within your area. Often times, visiting a dog show is a great place to interact with different breeders and to learn more about Boxers. Many breeders do something else for a living besides breed dogs, so don't be put off if you message one, and they don't immediately message you back.

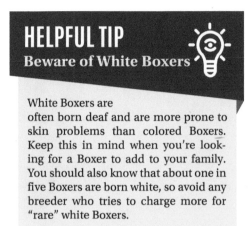

HELPFUL TIP

Beware of White Boxers

White Boxers are often born deaf and are more prone to skin problems than colored Boxers. Keep this in mind when you're looking for a Boxer to add to your family. You should also know that about one in five Boxers are born white, so avoid any breeder who tries to charge more for "rare" white Boxers.

You should never buy from a breeder without visiting their kennel or home. On the other hand, don't be totally put off if the whole place is not open to you. Breeders who care deeply about their animals want to protect them, and they don't know who may be carrying a disease. At the same time, you should be free to see the pups and at least one of the parents. Taking a good look at the parent often gives you important clues on what your future Boxer will be like.

Watch the interaction between the breeder and the dogs. You should see eager anticipation as the breeder approaches the dog. If you don't, consider that a red flag as it can be an important sign that the breeder is not properly caring for the animals. If you and the breeder both have children, then make sure to watch the interaction between the children and the Boxers when possible.

While it is impossible to keep an area where puppies are being raised impeccable, the area should be reasonably clean. If you are instantly turned off by odors coming from the area, then this is a sign that the pups are not being cared for, as odors can be a sign of infection. Dirty conditions may also signal a lack of care. For many breeders, Boxers are their passion. These individuals commit a lot of time and energy to his breed because they love their dogs, and not just because they want to make money off of them.

Good breeders are professionals who can teach you more about the breed. Reputable breeders would prefer that you get a dog that will thrill you for many years to come, even if they cannot make a sale on a given day. Good breeders care about their pups' outcomes, so they should not be too eager to sell their dogs. They want to educate their buyers so their pups have a good chance at having a great life.

Photo Courtesy of
Deborah Rothwell

Researching Breeders

It is impossible to overstate the importance of going to a dog show when possible before you get your Boxer. You can often visit with various breeders who should be willing to share their knowledge with you. This is particularly vital because the breeder that you ultimately buy from should be interested in making you an informed buyer, because then they know that their pup is likely to become a valued member of your family.

If that is not possible, then look at the American Boxer Club website. They have a breeder referral program that can help you find breeders in your area that are members of their club.

Some people turn to the internet to find breeders. Be very careful when choosing this technique since puppy mills often put a lot of effort into running their website to attract buyers. If you are going to look on the internet, then pay special attention to reviews left for the breeders. While every breeder can tell you a horror story about working with one buyer, if the majority of reviews are not positive, then quickly move ahead to another source. Breeders should be interacting with their buyers, sharing their knowledge as they should have a commitment to making the Boxer breed stronger. Don't be afraid to set up appointments to meet with different breeders. If you visit a breeder and your gut tells you that they're not a good choice, you're under no obligation to buy from them. Oftentimes, breeders will want to stay in contact with their buyers, so choose someone you would be willing to keep in contact with. Good breeders have a wealth of knowledge about Boxers and can be a fantastic resource for you to use in the future.

There are several things that you get when you use a reputable breeder that you do not get with most adoption agencies including health tests, guarantees, and contracts. These extras will help ensure that you're getting your money's worth and that your dog is expected to be healthy.

Health Tests and Certifications

Your chosen Boxer breeder should perform several health tests on the puppies and dogs before selling them. The American Kennel Club recommends that breeders perform the following health tests on Boxers:

Hip Evaluation - The most common hip evaluation tests must be done by a veterinarian and are sent to the Orthopedic Foundation for Animals for grading. Hip dysplasia can be a genetic trait that occurs when the leg bone does not fit properly in the socket. This condition can be passed on by the parents to offspring, so ask to see copies of the parent's screenings. While this is a great place to start, proper testing on individual animals cannot be done before they are two. Even then, injuries can lead to hip dysplasia without any genetics being involved.

Elbow Evaluation - Like hip evaluation, the Orthopedic Foundation of Animals offers testing for elbow dysplasia, and you should also ask to see these tests on the parents before making a purchase. Boxers are prone to three different types of elbow dysplasia that can be passed on genetically. This is a similar condition to hip dysplasia, but it affects the front legs.

Thyroid Evaluation - Hypothyroidism is fairly common in Boxers, and it can be passed on genetically. The condition can lead to obesity, which makes it doubly important to monitor a dog's diet if he is diagnosed with the disease.

Cardiovascular Tests - These tests look for genetic components to heart disease. The most common, although still rare, of these diseases is Boxer cardiomyopathy where the heart suddenly stops working properly. There is a genetic component, so make sure to see the parent's health tests on this one.

Degenerative Myelopathy DNA Test - This test looks for the onset of degeneration of the spinal column causing paralysis. These tests can come back normal, as a carrier allowing the dog to pass on the problem to offspring or at risk of developing the problem themselves.

If the breeder is unable to produce copies of these tests or is unwilling to show them to you, then you are not dealing with a reputable Boxer breeder. It is better to move on down the road before you discover that you have purchased a lifetime of health problems when you bought your dog.

Photo Courtesy of Laurie Roberson Topline Boxers

Breeder Contracts and Guarantees

One of the advantages of getting your Boxer from a breeder is that most offer breeder contracts and guarantees. It is vital that you read all documents carefully. If you have any questions, then be sure to ask the breeder before completing the sale. Reputable breeders should be more than happy to answer any questions.

Most breeders have developed their own contracts as there is no standard form across the industry. The overall purpose of the contract should be protection of the animal that you are purchasing. The contract should be written so that it protects both the buyer and the seller.

Normally, the contract will include the bill of sale. This shows that you paid the breeder or a person acting on their behalf for the dog. In some states, there are very specific laws about returning your dog within a few hours if the animal is sick. Other times, the bill of sale will state the conditions that the Boxer must be kept under, such as inside as a family pet.

Your contract should also say where the dog is registered. This is normally with the American Kennel Club, but it may be with another organization. While the seller will complete much of the information, it is up to you to see that it is filed and to pay the fee.

The contract may also include a statement that the dog is healthy when you get it. Furthermore, the contract may state that you need to tell the seller of any health concerns that arise, because reputable breeders track this information, allowing them to stop breeding any Boxer who is consistently producing offspring with health problems.

Breeders are interested in seeing that only the best animals have a chance to produce offspring, thereby helping to reduce the number of animals that are dumped each year. Therefore, the contract may include clauses that you will not breed the dog and that you will get it spayed or neutered as soon as possible.

If you are buying the dog to show, then the contract often becomes very elaborate as far as what you can do with the animals. This is because the American Kennel Club and other organizations have enacted rules that must be followed by those participating in their sanctioned events.

Do not be surprised if one of the clauses in the contract requires you to inform the buyer of what happens to the dog if you become unable or unwilling to take care of it. Many breeders love their animals so much that they will take a dog back if the buyer is no longer interested in caring for it. Many breeders have a clause where they will only refund the money within a given period, but they will always be willing to take the dog back.

Choosing the Perfect Pup

When it comes time to choose a Boxer puppy, it often comes down to the one that wins your heart the most. Many buyers report that they set out to buy the perfect Boxer only to discover that they find the one animal that they simply cannot leave behind. That is usually the one to take home and the best Boxer pup for you.

Even without veterinary expertise, a quick visual examination may help you spot a sick dog. The animal's eyes should be clear and there should not be any discharge around them. Have someone do something unexpectedly where the Boxer can barely see it. The dog should instantly turn their head towards the movement. Look at the ears for any sign of discharge and take a good sniff of them. Any signs of discharge or odor can be a sign of infection. The nose should be slightly moist without any signs of discharge. While the Boxer may be slightly excited, there should be no signs of excessive sniffling and no coughing. While it may feel a little gross, look at the dog's back end. Make sure that there is no runny discharge. If possible, wait for the dog to poop. It should be brown and in a lump. Runny discharge often indicates the dog is sick. Look around the case for any signs of diarrhea. If you suspect the puppies are not healthy, it is best to delay your purchase until you find ones that are healthy, as vet bills can add up quickly.

It's important to select a dog based on their temperament. Overly shy or timid dogs may display fearfulness as adults. The puppy that is always surrendering to his siblings may have a hard time getting to know other dogs because he doesn't feel secure. On the other hand, the dominant dog that is constantly being a bully to the other pups may seem playful but may also cause you problems with your other dogs if he always has to be in charge. The needy puppy is cute and affectionate, but could deal with separation anxiety as an adult. When choosing your pup, choose the one that is playful, but not aggressive, curious, but not needy. A puppy that is in the mid-range of dog temperaments is usually a good choice. If you can't tell all of this information from a meeting, ask the breeder about their personalities. They may be able to match you with the right dog.

When visiting the Boxer puppies, you may be tempted to take two puppies home so your dog has a friend. Especially if you are a first time Boxer owner,

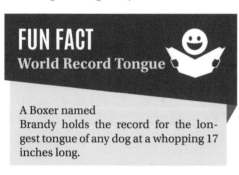

FUN FACT
World Record Tongue

A Boxer named Brandy holds the record for the longest tongue of any dog at a whopping 17 inches long.

buying littermates may be a mistake. Oftentimes, littermate owners have a hard time training their pups because they get too distracted by each other and fail to listen to their owner. Littermates are often more susceptible to separation anxiety if one needs to be separated from the other. Because littermates have never had to go without a sibling, they have a hard time coping if they are ever alone. If you want to have two Boxers, it may be best to raise a puppy until adulthood before adding another to the family. This way, you're not completely overwhelmed with raising two pups, and you don't have to worry about "littermate syndrome."

Regardless of whether you get a pup or an older dog, following this advice can help you pick out a healthy animal. Do not be afraid to trust your intuition. If you do not enjoy spending time with a breeder, you may want to look elsewhere. If their breeding operations are not clean or humane, it is important that you do not support their business. Regardless of what people tell you about buying or adopting, you're the one making the decision to bring a new family member into your home, so do what is best for you!

CHAPTER 3
Preparing Your Home for Your Boxer

Before you bring your Boxer home, you need to prepare your home, outdoor living space and yard. Boxers are prime investigators, and you do not want something happening as soon as you get the dog home. Just as if you were childproofing your home, you need to get on your hands and knees and crawl around your home looking for things that your Boxer may try to investigate.

Preparing Your Humans

"We always tell our new owners that it is seriously like having a baby all over again. Puppy proof EVERYTHING: from cords, plants, and anything that is on the floor. They will chew on shoes, wood, plastic and even metal at times!"

Brad & Gail Quistorff
Breezy Boxers

Photo Courtesy of
Patricia Densten

While your Boxer will probably earnestly desire to be in the middle of everything, it is important that you teach family members to treat the Boxer with respect. Children can seem intimidating to Boxers who are not used to being around them. It is best to introduce your Boxer to your children one at a time and teach them the proper way to behave around a dog.

Before you bring your puppy home, you may want to take anyone who lives in your home to the breeder's home to meet the new puppy. That way, your puppy can acquaint himself with people he will be spending time with. This is especially important for children who are not used to being around dogs. Remember, an adult should always be present when dogs and kids mix. Even a nice dog can nip at a child if the dog feels overwhelmed or scared. Teach children to pet a dog's back and avoid sensitive areas like the eyes, ears, nose, or tail. Tell your children to be gentle with the dog and never grab or hit him. If your child is too young to treat your dog gently, never allow your child to be alone with your dog, for both your child's and your dog's safety.

When your children interact with the Boxer in these early days, have the child sit on the floor with a special dog toy or treat. Then, let the Boxer decide if they want to approach the child or not. Remind the child to remain calm as the dog approaches even if they want to squeal with delight. As the dog approaches, then let the child give them the treat or try playing with the toy with them. Keep the session short and give the dog an out if the situation becomes overwhelming for them. While it is natural for the child to want to hug and kiss on the Boxer, this can intimidate some dogs in the beginning. Allow the child to pet the Boxer on the back if the dog seems accepting. It is very likely that soon the child and the Boxer will become almost inseparable.

A pet is a great lesson in responsibility and how to care for others. If your child is old enough to take on such chores, include your kids in your dog's daily routine. Teach kids how to supply your dog with the proper amount of food and fresh water. Remind them to tidy the house so the Boxer doesn't accidentally eat something he shouldn't. Have your kids take your dog to the backyard to play fetch—this is good exercise for both kids and dogs. Older children can also be responsible for taking the dog out and cleaning up his waste. Make sure you always double-check that your children completed their chores so your dog doesn't go hungry or miss a bathroom break. Otherwise, kids can be a great help and learn a lot about taking care of another living creature!

*Photo Courtesy of
Joelle Bezanson*

Preparing Your Pets

Fur children will also need to be prepared for the new arrival. While you can't sit your cats down and tell them to be nice to the new puppy, there are a few things you can do to make sure your new Boxer's transition is safe for every animal in your household.

Space is important. When animals are not comfortable around one another, they may try to separate themselves in order to calm down and feel safe. When your living situation causes your pets to be in close contact, you increase the chance for an altercation. For instance, your puppy may want to sniff your cat and your cat may not be interested in being bothered by an overly energetic dog. The cat will likely react by swatting your dog with her sharp claws. Or, some dogs with a high prey drive get too excited and want to catch a cat. Your dog may not understand that these other animals are not prey and it could have disastrous results. If you are not directly supervising your pets, find ways to create space. If you have caged critters, keep them in rooms that are off limits to your curious dog. Cats do well when they can hide in cat trees or can hop over gates and find shelter in a safe room.

The first time you introduce your new Boxer to your dogs, be careful not to force them to interact. Let your dogs sniff each other and give them time to slowly approach the other. Never push them to play; instead, allow them to interact organically. Otherwise, your dog may feel threatened. If your dogs do not get along during this first meeting, give them space and try again at a later date. It may take a few visits before your dogs are friends. Also, some adult dogs do not have patience for puppies. Puppies can be annoying to adult dogs because they haven't had the chance to learn how to act around other dogs. It is normal for an adult dog to avoid or act a little grouchy towards a puppy that is trying to nibble or jump on him. If your dogs begin to act aggressive, separate them immediately before any harm is done.

To give your dogs the best chance at having a successful meeting, try to meet in a neutral location. Your dog may not be happy if you bring a puppy into his house and let the puppy play with his toys and drink from his water dish. Some dogs can be very territorial and do not want an intruder to leave his scent in the house. A park or a friend's house are good first meeting locations because neither dog has claim to that location. Once your dogs successfully meet in a neutral location, have them interact again in your home.

Photo Courtesy of Brynn Holic

Giving the Boxer Indoor Space

"Don't allow your puppy to roam the entire home, find a smaller area/room to confine him/her to with gates. Ideally away from carpet, and keep anything you don't want chewed out of reach as well. This will make house training much easier."

Melissa Looman
Country Hill Boxers

Your Boxer needs space inside of your home. Boxers can get cold easily because they only have a thin coat. Additionally, Boxers are extremely susceptible to the heat. In fact, they can easily pass out if they get too hot. If you're looking for an outdoor dog, this is not the breed for you. Boxers need to be able to escape the elements and spend time with their people.

One way that you can take care of your Boxer is to create a special space for him. Find an area of your house where people generally spend their time, like the kitchen or living room. This is the room where you'll want to put your dog's bed or crate. Some dogs like the security of a "nest," so a corner of the room is a good place for a bed. This way, your dog doesn't feel left out of the family. Keep some toys nearby so your pup always has something to gnaw on.

If your new Boxer is not housetrained, you may want to find a way to contain him in an area with washable floors. A kitchen is a great spot because it is often near a back door and the floors are easy to wash. Set up a playpen or close off open doorways with baby gates so your pup cannot wander the house. In this space, place newspaper or puppy pads on the floor to make cleaning up accidents quick. Add a food and water dish and a couple of your dog's favorite toys to keep him occupied when you're not able to give him attention. This is a great setup for when you're away from home or you're busy and cannot keep direct attention on your dog.

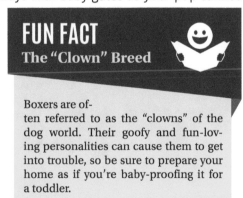

FUN FACT
The "Clown" Breed

Boxers are often referred to as the "clowns" of the dog world. Their goofy and fun-loving personalities can cause them to get into trouble, so be sure to prepare your home as if you're baby-proofing it for a toddler.

Photo Courtesy of Diane Majrowski

Getting Your Yard Ready for Your Boxer

"Check the safety of your yard for places of escape, poisonous plants, things that could injure your pup and if you have a pool, never leave your new pup alone in the yard."

Kathryn Brown
Codman Hill Boxers

Even though Boxers have trouble handling the heat and the cold, you will still want your new pup to play outside with you and your family. Therefore, it is essential that you prepare your yard. Remember that the Boxer is an investigator and even if you think you will keep a close eye on your dog when outside, it is best to prepare your yard for the Boxer before he gets into the street and gets hit, eats something bad for him, or has a run-in with the neighbor's cat.

Take a serious look at your yard before you bring your Boxer home so that you can remove all the things that might harm him. This includes fertilizers that are not pet friendly. One of the most common fertilizers that dogs get into is bone meal that is often put onto flower beds and gardens. If your Boxer gets ahold of bone meal, then it can cause iron toxicity that sometimes leads to harmful consequences. All fertilizers used on the yard need to be pet-friendly or you need to figure out a way to keep the Boxer out of that area. Additionally, car supplies, like de-icer and antifreeze, can harm or kill your Boxer. If you allow your dog to have garage access, place these items on high shelves where your dog cannot reach them.

One of the hottest trends in landscaping is to incorporate a water feature. If you have one of these, ensure it doesn't develop algae, as this can be deadly to your Boxer.

Look at any mulch in your yard. If you have used cocoa bean mulch, you need to remove it. When the warm sun hits this mulch, it produces a fragrant smell that your boxer is likely to love. Unfortunately, if he decides to eat it, then it can be toxic, cause diarrhea or vomiting.

You also need to think about what types of plants are in your yard. Some common plants are toxic to dogs. This includes many different varieties of mushrooms, but it can also include tulips, daffodils, and azaleas. In order to be safe, identify every type of plant in your landscaping and find out if it is harmful to your Boxer. Replace those that can be harmful to prevent further problems.

Your Boxer can also be an escape artist. You already know that this breed is great at agility, and he can climb or jump over a fence as soon as you turn your back. Your best bet is to install a solid panel fence that is at least six feet high. Chain link fences are usually a bad idea as your Boxer will just learn to climb them.

The investigative nature of Boxers makes them great escape artists if you decide to put them outside for a little while on nice days. As a responsible dog owner, it was important that I install a fence that made it hard for dogs to get out and keep it in good repair.

You have several different options in the type of fence that you want to use. Many people choose to use a chain link fence. If this is your choice, then make sure that your boxer cannot jump over the top of the fence. You will also want to run a row of barb wire at the bottom of the fence holding it in place with a thin trench filled with cement. In most cases, this will stop the dog from going up and over or down and under your fence.

Many people find, however, that their Boxer is agile enough to climb up a chain link fence. We once owned a black Labrador Retriever that climbed a nine-foot chain-link fence before we got him fixed. Remember that unneutered male dogs can smell a female in heat over five miles away. Besides getting this dog neutered, we quickly replaced the chain link fence with a smooth wooden fence that was high enough that he could not jump over it.

Other people choose to keep their Boxers in their yards by using an invisible fence. Wireless fences work by your dog wearing a radio transmitter that sends a small electrical shock to the collar whenever they leave the interior boundary of the fence. The second type is an in-ground system that gets buried underground. I am not a fan of these fences because they do nothing to stop other critters from entering my dog's space. I am also not a fan because I do not like to worry about my dog receiving a shock because the system malfunctions, which some are known to do regularly during lightning storms.

One of the best ways to make sure that your boxer stays in your yard is to make your yard dog friendly. Make sure to incorporate lots of activities that your dog will enjoy doing. Then, your dog will not become bored and try to figure out ways to escape. You should never leave your dog outside unless you are out there too because the boxer craves your companionship and can suffer from separation anxiety.

Necessary Supplies for Your Boxer

The upfront cost of a new puppy can be overwhelming, especially if this is your first pet. While there are some supplies like food and treats that you'll have to buy at regular intervals, there are some supplies that you may only need to purchase once. Try to pick up the essential supplies before your Boxer comes home so you won't have to worry about rushing to the pet store with a puppy in tow. Here are some supplies you'll want to have on hand for your new Boxer:

- Dog bed and/or crate
- Food and water dishes
- A sturdy collar and leash
- Identification tag
- Puppy food
- Treats
- A soft-bristled brush
- Toothbrush and dog toothpaste
- Nail clippers
- Dog shampoo
- A variety of toys and chews
- Playpen or gate
- Puppy pads

CHAPTER 4
Bringing Your Boxer Home

Once you have made the decision to get a Boxer, then it is important to develop a plan for the first few days. This allows everyone to feel more comfortable, including your Boxer.

The Importance of Having a Plan

It can take from two to eight weeks for you, your family, and your Boxer to become comfortable with each other. While you will love each other most of the time, there will be days when you wonder why you thought getting a Boxer was a good idea. Soon, however, you will have trouble remembering a time before you had your Boxer as they become a much loved member of your family.

Planning makes your life easier, which in turn makes your dog feel less stressed. Animals have a keen sense for when their human is upset, so feeling calm will help your dog feel calm. Preparing your home for your new Boxer is just one part of the plan—bringing your dog home and getting him settled in is the next step.

Photo Courtesy of Joelle Bezanson

The Ride Home

The best way to prepare for the ride home is to bring a crate with you to pick up your Boxer. Choose a crate that is approved by the International Air Travel Association as these will withstand most crashes if you are involved in one on the way home. The crate should be large enough that the dog can stand up, lie down, and sit down comfortably. While the exact choice of crate is up to you, if you think you will ever fly with your Boxer, then get one that has a sturdy roof and has food and water bowls that are refillable from the outside of the crate without needing to open the door.

While putting the Boxer in a crate for its ride home seems mean to some, it helps eliminate a lot of problems. The dog is contained in a safe space, so he is not trying to kiss you while you are driving down the road.

My daughter who was raised with dogs all her life did not follow this advice when she got her first dog after moving out on her own. Her dog managed to turn off the car without my daughter realizing it when she was driving down the interstate at 70 miles per hour. Thankfully, she was able to get the car to the side of the road, and it did not take her long to realize what had happened and get the car restarted.

If you have a loud and rambunctious family, then consider making picking up your Boxer alone or with a responsible adult. While the Boxer will soon be running with the rest of your family, it can be intimidating in the beginning. Give yourself and your boxer a break by creating a quiet ride home without any fighting over who gets to ride by the new pup or finger getting stuck in the cage.

The First Night Home

It is natural for both you and your Boxer to be anxious during their first night as your newest family member. It is important that you set the expectation that the Boxer puppy will sleep through the night in its own space. It is never a good idea to have the Boxer sleep in bed with you as you may startle it during the night, and the pup will snap at you before it's even awake.

Take the puppy outside before you go to bed. This is a great time to go for a walk or to play some active game to tire the puppy out. When the Boxer takes care of Mother Nature, then put the dog in the crate. You can put a cover over the crate to help the Boxer realize that it is bedtime. The crate should be placed in or near your bedroom allowing you to hear when the Boxer whines in the middle of the night to go outside.

Photo Courtesy of
Alyssa Schumacher

It is not unusual for a Boxer puppy to whine throughout the first night because he's frightened or confused. If you know that the puppy is okay, leave him alone. Do not give into the temptation to get the Boxer out to play or sleep with you, as you are setting the expectation for days to come. If you take your dog out in the middle of the night, make sure it's business only. Take your dog out without talking or playing with him and place him directly back inside the crate when you return. Especially in the early days, anticipate taking your pup out late at night, once in the middle of the night, and again in the early morning. You may need to go out even more, depending on your dog's age. Some estimate that a dog needs to go out every hour, depending on how many months old the pup is. So, a three month old pup would have to go out every three hours. However, every dog is different, and depending on your feeding schedule, you may be making more trips than that.

The first few nights home with your new boxer can be trying as the puppy learns to adjust to his role as a member of your family. Chances are that the pup will miss his mother and his litter mates if he is young. It is best that the pup learns to sleep in a crate near your bed. More than one owner has woken up to being snapped at by a dog they accidentally rolled onto while they were asleep.

You need to establish a bedtime routine. Early in the evening, take the Boxer outside for some exercise. This helps to ensure that the pup is tired and relaxed when it is time to go to bed. Once it is bedtime, then put the puppy in his crate. In the beginning, it is best to have the crate near your bed. Once the Boxer puppy is in the crate, then dim the lights and prepare for bed yourself.

If the puppy is still young, then chances are that he cannot hold his bladder all night. While it is best to put some puppy pads in the crate, most Boxers will not mess in their crates. Listen for your puppy to whine throughout the night so that you know that it is time to go outside. Generally, a puppy will need to go every four hours until he is four months old. Then, the amount of time that he can hold his bladder will increase about an hour each month until you both get to sleep through the night. Be careful to not give him too much attention during the night or the Boxer will start waking up just to play.

If your Boxer has a hard time settling down at night, there are a couple of different things that you can try. Have the puppy wear a pheromone-based calming dog collar. These collars are designed to smell like mother Boxers and may help your puppy feel more comfortable. You may also want to put a toy in the cage that the mother dog has played with in the past. Generally, if you give your Boxer puppy enough stimulation through the day, they will be prepared to sleep at night.

Keeping Your Boxer Comfortable at the Vet

It is essential that you take your Boxer to the vet as soon as possible once you've brought him home. If he is young, then he may need puppy shots and you are likely contractually obligated to do so if you bought him from a breeder. Regardless of age, you will want to establish a relationship with a great vet before something happens. You will also want to make sure that your dog is healthy. Discovering health issues early is a great way to help the Boxer live a long productive life, and it usually costs you less money to treat problems when they are little.

I love my vet. First, he is a very caring individual who has been supportive of my family and our community for many years. Second, he is extremely knowledgeable and not afraid to admit when he does not know something. Then, he will go searching for answers to improve the quali-

Photo Courtesy of
Nichole Edmonds

ty of my animal's health. He has been there when we have unfortunately had to make the tough decision to put some to sleep, and his compassion at that time was remarkable.

At the same time, it is my job to make sure that Zena, my Boxer, is ready to be seen by my vet. From day one, I have handled Zena all over. This helps me know what is normal and helps me spot problems sooner. Additionally, I have taught her to let me open her mouth and look in-

> ## FUN FACT
> **Famous Boxer**
>
> A famous Boxer in history was Sergeant Stubby, a war dog who became famous during World War I. He was the most decorated war dog of his time and the only one to become a sergeant. Sergeant Stubby fought in 17 battles, caught a German spy, and saved his fellow soldiers from a mustard gas attack. After he retired, he became the mascot for the Hoyas at Georgetown University.

side. Although Zena is extremely loving, I have also taught her to wear a muzzle even though she has never needed one. I am blessed to have a vet who lets me pay out my bills when they get too high. Every time that I go make a payment, Zena goes along. This helps her realize that going to the vet's office is a place where she gets lots of positive attention and treats.

Some dogs are wary of the vet; this is understandable because it can be a scary place with lots of strange smells, sounds, and touches. One of the best ways to make a positive connection to the vet is to give your Boxer treats along the way. Likely, your vet will also give treats to win your dog over. After your visit, reward your dog with something he loves, like going to the dog park or going on a walk on his favorite trail. You might even shop for a new toy or give your pup his favorite special treat. The more positive connections you can make, the better subsequent visits will be.

You can also work on making positive connections to things dogs may encounter during the visit to the vet to make them feel more comfortable before they even step foot in the clinic. For example, if your dog gets nervous on car rides, he may be a nervous wreck by the time you get to the vet. Practice spending time in the car for short periods of time until your Boxer willingly hops in. Some dogs do not like to be touched in certain ways, so mimic some of the exam steps at home. Run your hand along your dog's belly, have them hold still while you pretend to listen to their heart and lungs, look inside of their ears, and carefully lift their lips to examine their back teeth. If your Boxer can handle that, then he will be ready for the vet.

Educating Your Boxer

It is your job to educate your boxer. You may well discover that this is one of your favorite parts of the day as you and your dog enjoy each other's company. I know that it is one of my favorite parts, and as Zena's wolf pack leader, it is my responsibility to create training time almost every day. Of course, Zena is quick to remind me in case I forget, which tells me that she likes the time too.

One of the main problems that you may have with your Boxer is to get him used to playing nicely with other animals. Taking him to puppy school is a great way to get them used to being around other dogs. At the same time, make the most of your time in these classes by practicing the skills at home every day. Puppy classes do not teach your dog all of the important commands, but prepare your dog to learn in more advanced classes. Think of this as puppy kindergarten—this will help your dog develop skills that

Photo Courtesy of
Melissa Murray

will prepare him for training as an adult. Group classes allow your Boxer to interact with other dogs and people. Plus, it also teaches your dog that he must listen to you and look to you for direction. You may not leave your six or eight week course with a mastery of any obedience skills, but you've built a great foundation on which to build on.

Cost Breakdown for the First Year

Being the parent of a Boxer can be very expensive. In fact, I laughingly told my girls growing up that the dogs were another child and when money got tight, the dogs came first. While I am not sure that my girls believed me, I knew that they could get help from others while the dogs had no one to ask. Therefore, you need to think through the costs and prepare an emergency fund dedicated to caring for your Boxer. Some owners even like to purchase pet insurance, which is becoming more common through workplace insurance plans. Typical expenses during the first year include:

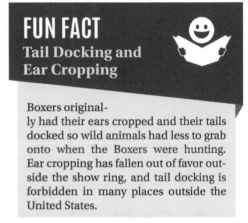

FUN FACT

Tail Docking and Ear Cropping

Boxers original-ly had their ears cropped and their tails docked so wild animals had less to grab onto when the Boxers were hunting. Ear cropping has fallen out of favor outside the show ring, and tail docking is forbidden in many places outside the United States.

While no doubt owning a Boxer is expensive, Zena and other dogs of this breed assure me that they are worth every penny that we spend on them. You know what? They are right! Their unconditional love is worth every penny that we spend on them to keep them healthy and happy.

CHAPTER 5
Being a Puppy Parent

"Boxers need and love their humans! They are a very social dog with their people and do not like to be left alone for long periods of times. Some dog breeds can get along fine not being around their humans a lot, but boxers LOVE their humans!"

Brad & Gail Quistorff
Breezy Boxers

You and your Boxer both have big roles to play in making sure that you can cohabitate. Your job is to be the teacher and your dog's job is to be the student. Just like all good teachers, you will need to find ways to keep your Boxer interested in learning new things. The great news that since the Boxer is both an investigator and eager to please you, your job is made much easier.

Photo Courtesy of Jessi Rich

Setting Realistic Expectations

You need to set high expectations that your Boxer will behave in the way that you want the dog to behave. Settling for less than the dog's best reinforces sloppy behaviors that will be even harder to break later. At the same time, you should be breaking tasks down into small steps that are easy to accomplish. Then, you can praise your dog and reward him often with small treats. This keeps him interested in learning. At the same time, keep training sessions short so that you do not try to train when your Boxer is tired. Try very hard to set aside at least 20 minutes each day to work with your dog.

It's also important to set realistic expectations for your feelings towards being a pet parent. Puppies are fun, but they're also a ton of work. It's easy to get frustrated when you want to sleep through the night but your dog wakes you up with his whining. Or, you may have plans to take your dog on a nice walk, only to have your puppy drag you in every direction for the whole trip. It's undoubtedly frustrating when you cannot reason with an animal who seems to make his own rules. Having a dog in the family is a gift, but it does not come without minor inconveniences. Set realistic expectations for what life with your Boxer will be like. The ability to stop and take a deep breath when things are not going well will serve you well during the early years with your Boxer.

Many Noises

If you think that you have gotten a quiet dog when you bring your Boxer home, then you are in for a real surprise, as most Boxers are far from quiet. Understanding what they are trying to tell you, if anything, can help you be a better Boxer parent.

You may hear your Boxer puppy moan frequently. If he is surrounded by someone he loves, then he is telling you that he is extremely content and happy. This, however, is not true if the Boxer is lying down with his eyes half open. Then, the dog is hoping that you are going to play with him, but he is assuming that you are not going to right then.

You may also hear your Boxer whine. If the whine rises in pitch, then you need to try to figure out what is bothering your four-legged friend. If the whine stays at the same pitch or gets slightly deeper at the end, then he is telling you that he is excited about something. Perhaps, he is telling you that he hopes it is playtime soon.

Additionally, your Boxer may growl. If he is growling and showing his teeth, then something has made him angry. On the other hand, if you cannot see his teeth, then the pup probably just wants to play.

One sound that the Boxer makes frequently is a farting sound. While this is perfectly normal in all dogs, many Boxer farts are extremely loud. If your Boxer decides to fart when you are around, you may want to quickly move to a different area of the room.

While I have not had any problems with Zena barking at the wrong time, I have had this experience with other dogs that I have owned in the past. Remember that Boxers can hear a lot that we cannot hear with our human ears. Since they are very protective, accept that they will bark to warn you that danger may be approaching, even if it is the trash truck over 10 blocks away!

Photo Courtesy of
Nicole Prevost

Common Puppy Problems

Puppies have the tendency to be naughty. This isn't entirely their fault because they are still learning how to behave. If your new Boxer pup is a pain in these first few months, he's not defective! It's perfectly normal to have a dog that is into everything for the first year (or longer) of his life. You'll want to correct these things as you observe them, but know that it's a puppy's nature to make a mess while exploring the world around him.

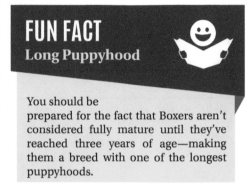

FUN FACT
Long Puppyhood

You should be prepared for the fact that Boxers aren't considered fully mature until they've reached three years of age—making them a breed with one of the longest puppyhoods.

Biting is very common in puppies because dogs use their mouth like humans use their hands. Your puppy has not figured out that their sharp teeth hurt, so he doesn't see anything wrong with clamping down on your toes. Plus, teething is uncomfortable for dogs and they will want to chew on something to relieve that irritation. If your Boxer puppy does not have toys to chew on, he will nibble on shoes, furniture, and just about anything lying around. There are a few ways you can prevent this behavior. If your dog nibbles on you, make a yelping sound. This tells your pup that his biting hurts. Because he doesn't want to hurt you, he'll take this cue and learn not to bite. To keep your dog from chewing on your belongings, the best way to avoid it is to keep everything out of reach and provide him with lots of different options for chewing. Expecting a puppy not to chew on something is completely unreasonable, so keep plenty of toys on hand.

Usually, dogs dig because they are trying to build an outdoor "nest" to relax in, are trying to escape, or are bored. These causes can be prevented once you figure out why your Boxer is digging.

Often times, dogs will dig when it's hot outside because it is cooler underground. Boxers overheat easily, so you might find your dog digging a hole under a bush to get some relief from the heat. One way to prevent your dog from digging for this reason is to keep him inside when it's hot, unless you're outside to supervise and correct him when he starts to dig.

Sometimes, dogs dig because they want to venture outside of the confines of your yard. This is a big problem if your fence has a gap. It won't take long for your determined puppy to create a hole large enough to slide under. If your Boxer likes to escape, you may want to build a fence that is par-

*Photo Courtesy of
Whitney Hacker
Sara Tiffany Photography*

tially buried underground. That way, if your dog starts digging, you may be able to fill the hole before your Boxer gets free. Adding more dirt or even landscaping stones around the fence line may deter your dog from digging an escape route.

Otherwise, your dog may dig because he's bored. Digging can be a fun activity that burns energy. But, because it is destructive, you'll want to put an end to it as quickly as possible. To prevent boredom digging, give your pet an outlet for his energy. Take him on a walk or toss a ball to him until he's too tired to play. That way, he'll be more likely to chill out on the deck instead of digging a tunnel underneath a bush.

Separation Anxiety

"A Boxer's favorite spot in the house is less than an inch from you, so don't turn around too quick."

Melissa Looman
Country Hill Boxers

Most Boxers really do not like being left alone. While it is a necessary part of life, you need to be proactive in helping your new pup feel as comfortable as possible when you leave, as separation anxiety can lead to depression and physical ailments. Additionally, your Boxer may decide that he is mad at you and be destructive. While I work from home, Zena used to cry horribly when I would leave her for about three hours every morning.

While it is difficult to find the middle ground, most Boxers do best when you confine them to a smaller puppy proofed space when you leave them home alone. If you put them in too small an area they may feel too confined and get even more depressed. If you leave them in too large an area they can become destructive. Therefore, leaving them in one room gives them the right amount of freedom. You may want to use gates to confine your Boxer to the kitchen or close a door leaving them in the laundry room.

You should also experiment to see if your Boxer does better near a window or where he cannot see outside. Some Boxers tend to quiet down and relax when they can watch the world pass by, while others do better when they cannot see outside because it overstimulates them.

47

Your dog should always have access to water. Additionally, many find that their boxer enjoys watching television or listening to the radio while they are gone. Choose music or shows that are relaxing and calming. Some owners record dog shows off the television and set them to replay throughout the day so that the Boxer doesn't feel alone.

Photo Courtesy of
Brynn Holic

It is vital to stimulate the dog while you are gone. After all, you would get bored lying in the same spot all day with nothing to do. Therefore, you will want to put out a few toys to encourage the dog to play throughout the day. In addition, you may want to use a dog-calming diffuser to help your Boxer relax.

While it is not always possible, at least in the beginning, you or another responsible individual should check on the pup every four hours. This helps to break up boredom throughout the day and ensures that your dog is doing okay.

You and your Boxer will have come a long way once you master the lessons in this chapter. Understand that it takes time and work. Reward small accomplishments and do not get too angry when your dog makes a mistake. After all, it is a learning process for everyone.

CHAPTER 6
Potty Training

Potty training your puppy will take a lot of time and energy. On average, it takes about four to six months to successfully housetrain a dog. Generally, Boxers are lovable dogs that are eager to please. It is your job as their owner to make sure that they behave. The great news is that most Boxers are so willing to please that potty training them is usually a very easy process. There are many things that you will need to train your Boxer to do including going potty in an appropriate place. Positive reinforcement is key to establishing a positive connection between proper behaviors and rewards.

Photo Courtesy of Joanne Elizabeth Dull

Options for Potty Training

"Plan on setting the alarm and taking your puppy out during the night to relieve themselves. A good rule to follow is for every month they are in age, that's the maximum number of hours they can go without a bathroom break until they reach 8 months old."

Melissa Looman
Country Hill Boxers

To begin, take your dog outside on his leash and direct him to a spot in your yard that will work well for a "toilet." The perimeter or a corner of your yard is a good spot because it will make cleaning up easier on you, plus dogs do not like to soil the areas they spend time in. Take your Boxer to the same spot each time because your dog's scent will remind them of the reason you took them out in the first place. Give them a little time to sniff around and do their business, then reward them when they go. A treat or a little bit of playtime before you go back inside can be very rewarding for a dog.

Because not every dog is the same, you may want to try different strategies for housetraining your Boxer. If one technique doesn't work for your dog, don't be afraid to try new things. Melissa Looman of Country Hill Box-

Photo Courtesy of Randi Hvarre

ers in Vermont says that she likes to potty train Boxers using a bell. She says, "My favorites are crate training and the bell. You can do a combination of the two, which works great. Every time you bring your puppy outside to relieve themselves, before opening the door ring a bell that is hung next to the door. In my experience, they catch on fast and before you know it you will hear the bell being rung for a potty request."

Many breeders stress the importance of sticking with whatever method your breeder has started. In almost all cases, that is crate training. Start by introducing the crate to your dog. Then, leave him in it for short periods of time. You and your Boxer will enjoy this time to unwind and get ready for the next activity together. The crate should never be used as punishment.

As soon as you take the puppy out of the crate, take him outside to go potty. If you are following Melissa's example, mount a bell down low and ring it before going outside. If your puppy goes, then give him a small treat and verbal praise. Soon, the Boxer puppy will understand that he needs to go potty outside to earn a reward.

If the puppy does not go immediately, then go back inside. Play with the puppy for 10 or 15 minutes. Then, take him outside again. Chances are that with all the activity the Boxer will now need to go. If not, then keep repeating the process until your dog eventually relieves himself.

Photo Courtesy of Linda Meeks

Another option that some people use is to paper train the boxer. Decide on where the Boxer's safe area is going to be. This can be a crate or a room. Line the entire area with puppy pads. As soon as the puppy goes on the pad remove the soiled pad. After you are sure he has the idea, then start picking up one pad each week. Soon, the Boxer will get the idea that he is supposed to go in a very limited area.

Still, others choose to train their Boxers to go in a litter box like a cat. Start by introducing the litter box to the puppy. Praise and reward the dog for being willing to walk in the box. Take the dog to the box every time that you take him out of the crate.

When your Boxer goes in the box, reward him. Soon, your pet will get the idea that going in the box earns him rewards. Since most Boxers are eager to please, most will get the idea rapidly. If you later decide to transition the Boxer to go outside, then try placing some litter on the ground to show your pup where you want him to go.

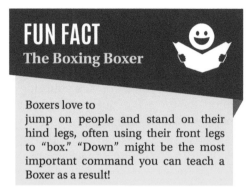

FUN FACT
The Boxing Boxer

Boxers love to jump on people and stand on their hind legs, often using their front legs to "box." "Down" might be the most important command you can teach a Boxer as a result!

Keeping it Positive

"Buy a crate and crate train your puppy. It's a safe place for them to rest when they are tired or if things are busy in your home and you cannot keep close watch on him/her. It also may prevent chewing of your furniture and aid in house training."

Kathryn Brown
Codman Hill Boxers

Potty training can be a trying time for a new dog owner because a puppy is bound to have accidents. The idea of going to a separate place to do their business is a completely foreign concept that will take some time to learn. Therefore, it's the owner's job to make learning as efficient as possible. The best way to train a dog is through positive reinforcement. That means that every time your Boxer goes potty outside, he gets praised and rewarded. A little treat or some playtime can be very rewarding for a dog, and praise and chin scratches let your dog know that he did something good. For at least the first year of your Boxer's life, give them praise every time they successfully potty outside.

If you come home to discover that your dog had an accident, there is no point in scolding or trying to punish him after the fact. Dogs will have a hard time connecting the mess on the floor to something they did. Rubbing your dog's nose in a mess while yelling at them won't remind them that they're not supposed to potty inside, but will upset them. If your Boxer is scared of you because you rubbed their nose on the carpet, they may still have accidents, but will be better about hiding them. If you find a pet mess, the best thing you can do is clean it thoroughly with an enzymatic cleanser so your dog doesn't smell the microscopic scent particles and potty in the same place.

The only time you can redirect your dog is while he's in the process of having an accident. If you see your dog starting to sniff or squat, get his attention and move him outside as fast as you can. If you couldn't catch him in time, clean the mess and try to take him out earlier next time. If your Boxer has a positive connection with pottying outside, then he'll be likely to give you his cues so he doesn't have to disappoint you. Plus, some dogs will do anything for a treat, so if your pup knows that squatting in the right place earns a reward, he'll do his best to make it outside.

Photo Courtesy of Allison Burnett

Playpens and Doggy Doors

A dog playpen may be the perfect answer for the times that you cannot carefully supervise your Boxer, but you know that they need exercise. You can use them inside when you want to let your Boxer out of his crate, but you have guests over that are leery of dogs, as they set a perfect boundary. These are effective for housetraining because dogs do not want to soil their living space. Like crates,

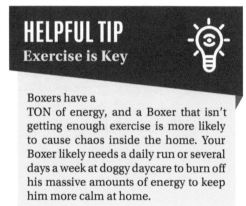

HELPFUL TIP
Exercise is Key

Boxers have a TON of energy, and a Boxer that isn't getting enough exercise is more likely to cause chaos inside the home. Your Boxer likely needs a daily run or several days a week at doggy daycare to burn off his massive amounts of energy to keep him more calm at home.

these will keep your Boxer from willingly soiling their space, while allowing for more movement.

Many Boxer owners wonder about installing a doggy door so that their Boxer can come in and out as they desire. While the dog may be able to let him in and out relieving himself as necessary, even if you are not home, and a doggy door can help stop boredom as the dog can play outside, doggy doors also come with disadvantages. Some Boxers do not realize when they are getting too hot or too cold, so they can die without supervision when they go outside. The biggest problem with dog doors, however, is that the inquisitive Boxer can find the hole in the fence and escape. Then, they may get run over, get picked up by authorities, or get into other trouble.

Additionally, if you are not an expert builder, then you may discover that you need six hands and a zillion tools to install a doggy door. If the door does not fit properly, then they may also raise your heating and cooling bills. And, the door is just large enough for small animals to climb into your house. If you live in an area with raccoons, squirrels, and skunks, there's a small chance these critters can enter your home, or your Boxer can drag one of his prizes inside.

In time, your dog will be perfectly capable of going outside to do his business. Until he has mastered that skill, be patient and keep lots of treats and cleaning supplies on hand. You may not be able to prevent all accidents, so expect to clean up some messes in the first few months. It can be frustrating to have a rambunctious puppy leaving waste all over the house, but it's important to be patient and clean up the messes so your Boxer won't keep making the same mistakes. With some positive reinforcement and a lot of trips outside, your dog will be potty trained in no time!

CHAPTER 7
Socializing with People and Animals

"Socialize, socialize, socialize. Take your puppy to puppy classes, walk in dog parks, have family and friends come over to meet the puppy with their dogs and go see friends and families at home with their dogs or other pets. Find a friend that has a dog and make walking dates. Find as many training classes as you can as your puppy grows."

Brad & Gail Quistorff
Breezy Boxers

One of the problems that you may encounter with your Boxer is that they love people. Some people, however, do not appreciate a 55 to 70 pound dog charging at them. Therefore, it is important to teach your Boxer how to behave around other people. Boxers are naturally social, but they need the right interactions at a young age to get along well with others. Socialization is necessary for your dog to be happy and safe around other people of all ages and different pets. This is best done when your Boxer is young, between three and seven months.

Photo Courtesy of Joelle Bezanson

Greeting New Human Friends

It only takes one unfortunate incident for a dog to mistrust strangers or certain types of people. This type of fear is often found in rescues because many have experienced trauma in their past home. However, dogs that are especially protective of their owners may act negatively towards others if they haven't been taught that humans are safe to be around. Little by little, expose your Boxer to all sorts of different people. Sometimes, dogs can be skittish around men, so invite your biggest friends to play with and cuddle your new dog, while offering tons of treats.

Photo Courtesy of Joanna West

Once you get your new dog, you're going to want to show him off to the world. However, ease into this process because some dogs can get overwhelmed with a lot of commotion and attention. When teaching your Boxer to interact with others, never force them to be close to someone. Instead, have a friend sit on the floor with some toys and treats. If your dog chooses to approach the friend, this is great. If not, you must respect your dog's distance. Your Boxer will approach the person when they are ready. Repeat this process with a variety of people, including children who have been taught how to interact with animals. If your guests are calm and quiet, your dog has no reason to fear your friends.

At the same time, it's important that you make sure others are not afraid of your dog. One of the things that many Boxers have trouble doing is greeting people appropriately. Their size and their almost endless energy mean many people are intimidated by them. Plus, these strong dogs often get a bad reputation of being mean, when they can be very sweet and loving dogs. It is your job to make sure that you keep your Boxer on good terms with most people by teaching them to greet others appropriately.

While this skill is extremely difficult for many Boxers to grasp, it is an essential one.

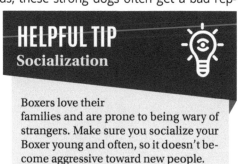

HELPFUL TIP
Socialization

Boxers love their families and are prone to being wary of strangers. Make sure you socialize your Boxer young and often, so it doesn't become aggressive toward new people.

57

Photo Courtesy of
Jami Andrus

The skill can be broken down into three different levels. In order to pass the first level, the dog must sit while their masters greet someone. During the second level, the Boxer must sit and be petted on the head or under the chin without breaking the sit. The third level, which is the one required for the American Kennel Club's Good Canine Award, requires that the dog walk next to their master while they greet another person leading a dog. The two people must then shake hands and carry on a short conversation before proceeding.

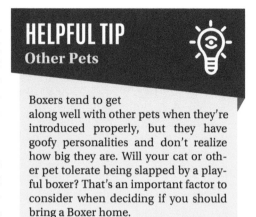

HELPFUL TIP
Other Pets

Boxers tend to get along well with other pets when they're introduced properly, but they have goofy personalities and don't realize how big they are. Will your cat or other pet tolerate being slapped by a playful boxer? That's an important factor to consider when deciding if you should bring a Boxer home.

Training for this behavior is like training for any other behavior. You must reward the behavior that you want to see while ignoring the behavior that you do not want to see. In the beginning, you will need your Boxer on a leash, and you will need a helper. Give the helper a dog treat. As the helper approaches tighten your hold on the leash so that your Boxer cannot jump. Then, have the helper hold out the treat above the dog's head. Since your Boxer will figure out that he cannot get the treat by jumping, he will sit down to figure out how to get the dog treat from the helper. As soon as he sits down, then give him the dog treat.

You will need to repeat this exercise until your Boxer grasps the idea that sitting down will be rewarded. If the Boxer chooses not to sit or jumps, then have the person approaching, turn his back and refuse to give the treat until the dog sits.

Zena and I spent quite a bit of time living alone, so there was no one else to help us master this. It is still a work in progress on some days, but you can train your dog to greet people appropriately without any help. Put your Boxer on a tether and fasten one end of the tether to a stationary object. Alternatively, you can put a hook on one end of the tether and shut it behind a door. Now, walk far enough away from your dog that he cannot reach you. Slowly walk toward him with a treat in your hand. If the Boxer tries to jump for the treat, then back up. Soon, he will figure out that he has to sit down to get the treat.

Now that you have the basic idea enforced in your Boxer's brain, go for a walk. When a friendly stranger approaches and asks if he can pet your dog, ask if he will help you. Give him the treat and tell him to give it to your dog, only if your dog stays seated. Most people will be glad to help you train your Boxer.

Interacting with Other Animals

After a while, most Boxer owners discover that they want another pet in their lives. It may be that they just want to take their Boxer to another dog owner friend's home or a local dog park for a playdate. On the other hand, they may be looking for another Boxer to add to their family. Still, others find that while they love their Boxer, they want to add another type of pet into their lives. It may be a cat, a rabbit, or even a ferret. Before you bring your Boxer around other animals, there are some tips that you need to keep in mind.

Make sure that your Boxer is fully vaccinated. In particular, you want to ensure your dog is protected against parvovirus. While dogs will not be fully protected until they finish their vaccinations around their first birthday, Boxers under five months are most at risk. It is best to avoid dog parks, pet stores, and other areas where dogs are allowed with your Boxer until he is fully protected.

If you have not yet adopted a Boxer, then make sure to introduce him to your pet family members before you agree to make him a member of your family. Just remember that while you are the owner, but your pets have a vote too.

Photo Courtesy of
Michael Ragusa

Introducing Your Boxer to Pet Friends

"I recommend having play dates at your home with other trusted, social dogs. Body language is taught and mimicked by other animals."

Jeannie McElroy
Big Mac Boxers

Playdates can be fun for you and your dog. These introductions are best accomplished on neutral ground as one dog may feel that he has an advantage if you are meeting on his territory. Many pet stores, shelters, and rescue organizations are happy to help you introduce your new Boxer to another animal.

The dogs should first be walked where they can see each other, but not close enough to be intimidated. If the dogs act like they don't even notice the other animal or just get along naturally, then give them a treat. Then,

Photo Courtesy of
Brenda Nutford

walk each dog where the other has walked so that it can smell the other dog's scent. If either dog seems apprehensive or afraid, then repeat this step until they seem relaxed.

Continue introducing the dogs to each other by letting one dog walk behind the other in a relaxed manner. If they stay relaxed, then give them a treat. Reverse the process allowing the other dog to take the lead. If all goes well and you are in a safe area, then take the dogs off their leashes allowing them to play together.

If either dog seems to be aggressive towards the other one, then put the dogs back on their leashes. Then, do a few obedience tricks with your Boxer and give him treats to get him to relax. Introduce the dogs to each other again. While some dogs instantly love each other, it may take a few meetings for other dogs to get along.

Throughout the process, you will want to be very aware of what your Boxer's body language is trying to tell you. If you see your Boxer bowing, blinking rapidly, or trying to lick the other dog's muzzle or ears, then he is trying to get the other dog to pay them attention. Any sign that your dog is not moving normally may indicate that he is fearful. While some Boxers yawn to show that they are tired, other dogs yawn when they are afraid. If you see your dog attempting to look smaller than he is, then he perceives a threat. This can be especially true if the Boxer's tail goes low and he is actively turning his head away from the other animal.

There are several behaviors that you want to see when you are introducing two dogs to each other. One of them is the tongue sticking out and rolling from one side to the other. Boxers are notorious for wiggling their whole backside when they are happy and excited. They may also blink their eyes repeatedly at the other dog.

Photo Courtesy of Emily Entrop

Pack Mentality

Boxers, like most dogs, have a pack mentality. The better that you understand this mentality, the more successful you will be at training your dog because you will be a better pack leader.

Set boundaries indicating that you expect your Boxer to obey the rules and stay in his space. Your dog should not be constantly trying to jump on you unless you choose to teach him to give hugs. The Boxer should understand that you own the space and part of his responsibility in sharing it with you is to follow your rules.

Photo Courtesy of
Laurie & Mike Wigginton

Give your dog a job and expect that he will carry it out faithfully. You should regularly be training your Boxer, as learning is part of his work. You may also want to play interactive games with your dog or take him to run errands with you. Rotating out toys so that there are often ones that he has not seen for a while makes Zena work to remember how to play with them. There are even toys that you can hide treats in, but I have gotten these for Zena, and she is not fond of them. The point is that your Boxer should be expected to use their mind every day for something.

While it is your job to give your dog high quality dog food and treats, it is your dog's job to be calm while you are preparing his meal. There are very few things worse than a 50 plus pound monster bouncing around while you are trying to get their dog food out.

Raising Multiple Boxers

Dogs are social animals, and they may really enjoy playing with each other most of the time. Unless you set clear expectations, however, you can expect some issues to arise unless you take control of your dogs. I once had six dogs who all got along peacefully 95 percent of the time.

One of the keys to living peacefully at our house was that each dog had its own eating space. Two dogs ate in opposite ends of the kitchen, one in two different bedrooms, and two outside. They each knew where their food dish was and did a decent job of leaving each other's food dish alone.

The second key to living peacefully was to teach the dogs to sit and stay until they were released. The sit-and-stay command is particularly useful for controlling movement within your home.

If there was conflict among the dogs at our house, it usually happened during playtime. One way that we solved this was to put the dogs in their crates with a favorite toy. Then, we took one or two dogs out at a time for play and training. Eventually, everyone figured out that they were going to get their turn if they were just patient enough. In fact, most of the time, we took out the quietest dog first, and I am pretty sure that the other dogs realized that if they were patient, their turn would come sooner.

Boxers Who Hate Other Pets

Maybe it is the fact that Zena was found on the side of the road after being dumped and then taken to a home where she was not accepted, but Zena still has trouble accepting other animals.

The first step in getting Zena to the point where she would come and sit at my heels when she saw another dog was to teach her to associate doing the right thing to get a reward. I would carry a pocketful of her favorite treats when we would go for a walk. Then, when I spotted another

Photo Courtesy of
Amber Simmons

dog, I would give her the command to focus and reward her with a treat when she did.

Soon, Zena figured it out. If she saw another dog and focused on me, then a treat was coming. Since she really loves her treats it did not take her long. Then, I worked on shaping this behavior so that she would come stand beside me when she saw another dog. The next step was to teach her to sit down using her favorite food rewards.

While our walks may take longer than many dog's walks, I am not constantly fighting with her when the neighbor's dog decides to run up to her. Therefore, it becomes a win win for everyone.

If your dog's aggression towards other pets or your other pet's aggression towards your new Boxer is putting anyone at risk, you must make a decision on how to move forward. At first, you may try intensive training to work with your pet's aggression. Find a private trainer who has experience with these types of problems to work with your dog. They may be able to find a solution to your particular problem.

If training and socialization doesn't help, you may need to rehome a pet. This can be an extremely difficult thing to do, but it's worth it if your pet can find a new home where everyone is safe. If your new Boxer has not been welcomed by your other pets and you fear for his safety, you may need to return him to the breeder or shelter. You may not get any money back, but the breeder or shelter would rather the dog is safe with them, than in a house that could be dangerous. Or, if you've had trouble with an old cat that doesn't take to new pets and you really want the Boxer, you may find a new home for your grouchy kitty that doesn't have any other pets. These decisions are tough, but not as tough as coming home to a pet that has been seriously injured or traumatized.

Oftentimes, new owners get so fixated on housetraining and obedience training that they forget to socialize their Boxer. However, this is an extremely important part of raising a dog. Ideally, this is done in the first few months of when you bring your dog home; it's still important to help your Boxer feel comfortable around others, even if he's an old rescue dog. Create positive interactions between your dog and different types of strangers—both human and animal—and your new Boxer will be much more at ease and easier to handle.

CHAPTER 8
Physical and Mental Exercise

"A happy dog is one that has had plenty of exercise, and happy dogs tend to not get into so much trouble. I highly encourage large fenced in yards for boxer owners. We are constantly letting our dogs in and out all day long. They don't usually like to be out for long periods of time unless you are with them every time, and that is not always convenient. Just taking a boxer for a walk is not enough. They need to run, jump, and be silly. The best exercise for them is off leash in a safe place."

Melissa Looman -
Country Hill Boxers

Exercise is an important part of your Boxer's daily routine. Without it, your dog will lose muscle mass, gain extra fat, and will be very bored and restless. While most dog owners assume a daily walk is enough, there are more things you can do to entertain your dog. In fact, mental stimulation is just as important as physical exercise. This chapter will give you some ideas for ways to boost your Boxer's physical and mental fitness.

Exercise Requirements

Your Boxer's exercise needs will vary depending on your dog's life stage. As a pup, your little dog will be a ball of energy for brief periods of time. A few short walks a day will give your dog enough exercise to start developing strong muscles without overworking him. Mix in a little playtime and your pup will get all the exercise he needs.

An adult Boxer needs slightly longer periods of exercise. If possible, try to take your dog on two walks a day. One of these walks can be brief, just long enough for your dog to stretch his legs and expend some pent up energy. The other walk should be at least 30 minutes long. In between walks, supplement the exercise time with trips to the backyard to play fetch or Frisbee. Don't be surprised when your young adult Boxer still has energy after you've taken him on his walk—dogs this age love to exercise in short spurts.

Your dog may trail behind at the end of a long walk, but will want to play again after a short nap.

Senior dogs may not need as much physical exercise as young pups. Follow your dog's lead with this one. If he's eager to get outside first thing in the morning, continue walking as usual, but consider cutting walks a little shorter if he gets tired before you get home. Old joints may feel sore when jumping and running at full speed, so take it easy when you play fetch. Old dogs still want to be active and play, but be mindful of how your Boxer's body changes as he ages. You don't want to risk an injury because you didn't pay attention to your dog and pushed him too hard.

Remember to adjust your dog's exercise routines to his energy level. If your Boxer is a ball of energy, add more exercise until he's able to calm down while he's in the house. Or, if your dog is panting hard on your walk, start slow and build up distance as your Boxer gets into better shape. Always watch your dog's behavioral cues to know how to proceed. Also, make sure your dog is protected from the elements. In the summer, bring water on your walks and find shade if it gets too hot. In the winter, use protective clothing to keep your Boxer warm.

Photo Courtesy of Pat Carter

Photo Courtesy of
Eugenio Campanile

Physical Exercise

Let's face it—walking the same route day after day can get boring for both you and your pooch. But there are lots of other fun activities that can burn energy and keep exercise time exciting.

If you're trying to get into shape, running can be an effective way to help your dog burn off energy. However, it's important to know that Boxers are sprinters, not long distance runners. Anything over a mile or two will be too much for their bodies. When you first start running with your Boxer, don't go the maximum distance or you'll find yourself carrying your little friend home. Just like with humans, dogs need time to get into shape. Start slow and increase the distance over time. Before long, you'll be racing around the neighborhood—which is great when your dog has a ton of energy and you're short on time!

HELPFUL TIP

Be Mindful of the Weather

As much exercise as Boxers need, it can be tricky to meet their needs depending on your climate. Boxers don't tolerate heat well due to their short muzzles, and their short coat doesn't protect them well from the cold. If you live in an area that experiences temperature extremes, make sure you have ways to exercise your Boxer even when the weather sucks.

Boxers are playful dogs who love to use their powerful bodies to impress you. If you have a yard with a fence, fetch and Frisbee are two activities that will allow your dog to show off his athletic ability. Pet stores sell different types of balls for fetch, but tennis balls are also a dog favorite. If you know any tennis players, ask them for their old, flat tennis balls. Your dog won't know the difference and it'll save you some money. Catching and fetching aren't intuitive for all dogs, so practice throwing from a short distance until your dog figures it out. When fetching, dogs often don't want to give the ball back, so this is a good opportunity to practice "drop it." Once your dog develops these skills, you'll be able to launch the ball across the dog park and your Boxer will chase it down and bring it back to drop at your feet in a flash.

Frisbee can also be a fun form of exercise for an athletic Boxer. A Frisbee from a pet store may be easier for your dog to catch than a hard plastic one. Dog Frisbees are light and made with fabric or rubber so it won't hurt if you accidentally hit your dog with an errant throw. When teaching your Boxer to catch a Frisbee, give lots of praise and treats when he manages to catch the disc from a short distance. Then, increase the throwing distance until your dog eagerly anticipates you launching the Frisbee across the yard. You'll be amazed at how high your Boxer will jump to catch a Frisbee.

As evidence of their strength, Boxers often excel in dog weight pulling. In this sport, a Boxer is fastened with a special harness to a cart with small wheels on it. The event takes place on a carpet, to avoid damage to the dog's paws. As the competition progresses, more weight is placed on the cart. It takes time to develop skills as a weight pulling dog and most Boxers really love spending that time with their masters.

Competitively, this sport has several different classifications. For example, I have worked with my dog Zena to pull a double-axel wheel cart. Before we get ready to go to a competition, she must be able to pull eight times her body weight. She must also be able to consistently pull it three times in a row to advance. We are gradually working up to that point, but we still have a long way to go. Others who participate with their Boxers in this sport have them pull a rail cart. These Boxers must be able to pull up to 10 times their body weight along a rail system. Still others choose to train their Boxers to pull sleds in real or artificial snow. These Boxers must be able to pull three times their body weight.

Once a Boxer qualifies at a meet, he starts earning points based on the amount of weight that he can pull and the type of vehicle he's dragging. The winner is the dog who consistently pulls the most weight. This unique form of dog exercise can be a lot of fun for you and your Boxer. If this sounds like an activity you and your dog would be interested in, talk to your breeder or trainer about preparing for and competing in this sport.

Keeping the Boxer's Mind Alert

Mental exercise is also important for your Boxer's overall well-being. Bored dogs can be destructive because they have to do something with their excess mental energy and common bad behaviors like chewing, digging, and barking can be a lot of fun for a dog. But there are a lot of fun things you can do with your Boxer to strengthen his mind and entertain him.

For starters, obedience training can keep your dog mentally sharp. When training, your Boxer is constantly watching your cues to figure out what you want him to do. He might see training as a game because he has to complete a task in order to receive a reward. Once you've mastered the basics, continuing to teach your dog fun tricks can keep him active and mentally engaged. Keep training time short—20 minutes at a time is about the maximum you want to spend working on a skill. Otherwise, training is not as fun for your dog and can get frustrating.

There are different variations of hide and seek games you might want to try with your curious pup. The simplest is to hide a favorite toy or treat under a blanket and have your dog try to find it. It's fun watching your dog sniff and paw at a blanket in order to find the reward. If your Boxer knows the sit and stay commands, you can teach him to search for you. Have him sit and stay in one room. Then, hide in another room and call your dog. He'll search every room in the house looking for you. Remember to give your dog a reward once he locates you. If your dog gets good at finding you, hide a toy in the house and tell your dog to find it instead. This is trickier because your Boxer cannot use the sound of your voice to locate the item. These are entertaining games that are especially good to play when the weather isn't right for being outdoors.

There are all sorts of different puzzles sold at pet stores that your Boxer may also enjoy. Some toys are filled with other plush toys for your dog to hunt down and chomp on. Other toys have moving parts that require precise snout movements to release treats. Some look like plastic or rubber balls that can be filled with food that require your Boxer to manipulate them in just the right way to make the food fall out. If your dog is food driven, these puzzles can keep him thinking in creative ways in order to get a tasty treat.

Photo Courtesy of Amber Simmons

Occupying Your Boxer When You are Busy

Between work, chores, and other daily tasks, it's impossible to keep an eye on your dog 24 hours a day. Therefore, you need a plan for how you're going to manage your Boxer while he's not under direct supervision.

In order to keep your dog well behaved while you're busy, you'll need to plan ahead. If you're entertaining guests for dinner, take your dog on a long walk or trip to the dog park a few hours prior. That way, he'll be too tired to bother you while you're cooking and cleaning. If your Boxer gets restless when you leave for work and wreaks havoc on your furniture, a brisk morning walk and a puzzle full of treats will keep his energy levels under control and give him something to do immediately after you leave the house. Before long, your dog will be ready for a nap.

Whenever you cannot directly supervise your dog, make sure you provide plenty of toys and chews for him to play with. Chewing is a relaxing and entertaining activity for a dog. Some dogs will chew for hours at a time! If your dog can entertain himself with a chew toy, he'll be less likely to chew on your belongings. When you leave your dog unsupervised with toys, make sure that there is nothing that could potentially be a choking hazard. If there are certain toys that your Boxer enjoys but can easily destroy in an hour or two, save those for a time when you're able to keep an eye on him.

A well behaved and happy dog is one who has had plenty of physical and mental exercise. Daily exercise is a necessary part of raising a healthy dog. Once you get to know your new Boxer, you'll discover just how much exercise and attention he needs. You'll also figure out what his favorite activities are. Try different activities to find something your dog excels at and enjoys. Not only will your Boxer be entertained, but you'll enjoy the variety as well.

CHAPTER 9
Training Your Boxer

"They will test you, be consistent with training and house rules."

Kathryn Brown
Codman Hill Boxers

Dog training can be a daunting task if you've never worked with dogs before. Sometimes, owners expect their dogs to learn like humans learn. This ultimately results in frustration because dog brains are different than human brains and need to be trained appropriately. Once you understand dog cognition, training becomes easier. However, your Boxer has a mind of his own and while the breed aims to please, your pup will still test your patience. The most important thing you can do during dog training is to stay positive! With the right mindset and preparation, training your Boxer can be a lot of fun!

Photo Courtesy of Randi Hvarre

Setting Clear Expectations

Dogs do not understand varying conditions like humans do. For instance, if you tell children that they cannot sit on your couch while wearing dirty clothes, they will avoid that seat when they are muddy, but will innately understand that it's fine to sit on the couch if they're clean. However, if you allow your dog to sit on your couch after a bath, but scold him when he tries to jump on your couch after playing in the mud, you will have a confused Boxer. With enough reinforcement and repetition, dogs will learn how to follow rules—they just won't be able to understand exceptions to these rules.

Because of this, it's good to set clear rules for both your dog and the family to abide by. If you don't want your Boxer shedding fur on your bed, make sure you don't correct him for jumping on the bed one day and then change your mind and call him onto the bed a different day. Make sure that your family members know the rules so they don't undermine your training efforts. It's helpful to sit down with the other members of your household to establish rules for your dog and to discuss how you plan on enforcing these rules. That way, there is consistency in training.

This type of consistency should extend into training classes. Have your partner or children come to class with you so they can see the methods your trainer uses. That way, you'll all use the same words for the same commands. A human will understand the difference between "yes" and "good" but a dog needs consistency in the words being used both for commands and reinforcement.

Skinner Was Right: Using Operant Conditioning

Dogs learn best through operant conditioning. Basically, behavior is shaped by the reinforcements that follow an action. In B. F. Skinner's classic experiment, rats were given food in exchange for pressing a lever. Because the rats liked the outcome, they changed their behavior and pressed the lever frequently to get food. Similarly, dogs will repeat actions if there is some reward attached to the behavior.

Negative reinforcement also shapes behavior. This can be in the form of punishment or the absence of reward. For example, Boxers are eager dogs who might try to jump on people to get attention. If you turn your back to your dog when he jumps, you're not providing the reward that he's looking for. So, this will eventually teach your Boxer that jumping is not an effective behavior. If you reward your dog when he sits down in front of you and waits for attention, he may find that this behavior is much more rewarding than jumping.

Repetition is necessary for a dog to become conditioned. If you only practice a command a few times, your dog cannot be expected to hear the cue and do the command without more prompting. Dogs are conditioned when they practice the same behavior with the same cue and receive a reward. This can take weeks or months to nail and often require regular practice. Your Boxer may perform a behavior with the right kind of prompting, but it won't be a reliable behavior without a lot of practice.

These psychological concepts can be applied to every aspect of dog training. You are simply using the tools of reinforcement to shape your dog's behaviors.

The Best Reinforcements

Not every dog is motivated by the same rewards. When you start to train your Boxer, see if he is motivated by treats, praise, or toys. Of course, a dog can be motivated by several of these things. If you drop a piece of food and your dog doesn't wait until it hits the ground to devour it, then he's probably food driven. If he is constantly bringing you balls or ropes to play with, he's probably toy driven. Since this breed tends to be eager to please, your Boxer is likely to be motivated by praise and chin scratches.

Once you know what your dog likes, introduce the very best of these rewards at the right moment. For instance, if you give your dog the same treat after every good behavior, he might not be as excited about the treats each

Photo Courtesy of
Gina Giordano

time. So, when you introduce a difficult or important command, give him a special treat that will really catch his attention. I've found that small pieces of hotdogs are very motivating on special occasions. If your pup is toy driven, try treating your Boxer with a special squeaky toy when you train and keep it stored out of reach for general play, so it remains special. Use different types of rewards that fit the scenario. If your dog loves to play, make fetch into a training moment by teaching "take it" and "drop it." That way, your dog gets to chase the ball again once he completes the command. For "stay" and "come," treats work well because the scent of a special treat is hard to avoid. Once you get to know your Boxer, you will know which rewards will yield the best results.

*Photo Courtesy of
Melissa Murray*

Stay Positive

"Boxers are very easy to train if you do it correctly. Keep in mind they are very smart, a bit stubborn, and they get bored easily. Keep lessons short and consistent with a lot of positive enforcement."

Melissa Looman
Country Hill Boxers

Positivity is the key to shaping dog behaviors. Punishment can be ineffective because it creates unintended behavioral changes. If you scream at or swat a dog for barking, while that may keep the dog from barking, it can also terrify him, who doesn't understand that he was doing anything wrong. Frightened dogs are less likely to trust their owner, which is necessary for training. Fearful dogs may also distrust others, ruining their chances at being successfully socialized.

Punishment is not the same as correction. With correction, you get your Boxer's attention when he's doing something bad. Then, you redirect the behavior and reward him when he either stops the bad behavior, or displays good behavior. For example, some dog trainers suggest keeping a plastic bottle full of rocks on hand to use as a redirection device. When a dog does something naughty, like barking, the owner shakes the bottle to get the dog's attention. This sound is startling, but not frightening. Then, once the dog stops barking out of surprise, the owner rewards him for being quiet. Instead of teaching the dog that barking is bad, it tells the dog that not barking is good. When paired with a command like "no bark," the owner has essentially created an off switch for when their dog barks too much.

Unfortunately, punishment often turns into abuse. A well-meaning owner may swat at a dog when he misbehaves because the owner erroneously believed that punishment was an effective way to deter bad behavior. People commonly rub their dog's nose in a potty accident while scolding their dog because they believe it will teach him not to make those mistakes. Instead of teaching, punishments that involve pain, fear, or force can cause serious trust issues that are hard to repair. Under no circumstances should an owner ever spank or shove a dog to teach him a lesson. Dogs are sensitive animals that are unable to understand why their owner is causing them pain.

*Photo Courtesy of
Lisa Pasquariello*

Because dog training can be frustrating, it's easy for owners to slip into punishment mode out of anger. Humans and dogs do not think in the same way, so it can be hard to understand why your dog is not cooperating, even when you're doing everything by the book. However, it's necessary to remain calm, no matter how much your dog is getting on your nerves with his bad behavior or indifference to your commands. If training becomes too much, take a step back and try again once you (and your dog) have chilled out.

Hiring a Trainer

Especially if you're a first time dog owner, it can be very beneficial to work with a professional trainer. There are different types of classes you can try with your Boxer. Many owners start with a puppy class because it's a good way to socialize a dog with other dogs and humans, plus it helps owners learn the fundamentals of dog training. From there, basic obedience classes help you teach your dog how to sit, lie down, stay, and walk alongside you. These obedience skills teach your dog basic manners that will make living with a dog much easier. Once you pass these basic classes, there are all sorts of classes you can try with your Boxer. If your dog is particularly active, you might do well in an agility class. Or, you can get certified in Canine Good Citizen. There are even classes that teach your dog how to sniff out certain scents. If your dog loves to have a "job," taking classes can be a lot of fun for an eager to please Boxer.

If your Boxer does not do well in a group setting, you can also hire a private trainer. A private trainer may be good for an adopted Boxer that gets nervous or aggressive around other dogs. Or, if your dog has a behavioral problem that is severe or difficult to handle, a private trainer may be able to give you the personalized attention you and your dog need. Some dogs get too distracted in a group setting, and one on one time with a trainer may be worth it. Personal dog trainers tend to cost more because they are only working with one client and not an entire group, but in special circumstances, it is worth it.

When looking for a trainer, you want someone who believes in positive reinforcement. If a trainer seems too harsh around dogs or dogs seem to fear him, find a different trainer. Look for someone knowledgeable and friendly because they will be one of your greatest resources while training. Certifications and experience are important. If you don't know where to look for a trainer, ask your local Boxer breeder. They may know people who do an excellent job training. Veterinarians and fellow dog owners are also great sources of recommendations. If someone you trust likes a trainer, you'll probably like them, too.

Are You Doing it Right?

There comes a time in every dog owner's life when they look at their unruly dog and wonder where they went wrong. While it's easy to look at training failures as evidence of a clueless dog owner, more than likely, you're doing a fine job. Here are a few common concerns and ways to troubleshoot training woes:

My dog will only do what I want when I give him a treat.

You may need more practice. When dogs become conditioned, they will hear the cue and perform the command. It takes a lot of time and repetition to get to that point.

My dog just doesn't care about treats.

If your dog is uninterested in your offerings, try a moist treat with a strong scent. Hot dogs or canned tuna in small quantities may be enough to get your dog excited. Or, try training before meal times when your dog is at his hungriest. Also, try incorporating more play rewards. If your dog won't come to you for a treat, maybe he'll come running if you show him a favorite toy.

My boxer is doing something that could be dangerous and I don't know how to stop it.

Talk to a trainer right away. Running off, pulling too hard on the leash, or acting out around other dogs are all behaviors that need to be corrected as soon as possible. If you take group classes, ask your trainer if she has any ideas of how to fix your problem. Or, if it's something ongoing and difficult to correct, hire a private trainer to work directly with you and your Boxer on a set schedule.

I get frustrated when I train my dog because he doesn't listen. Should I keep training?

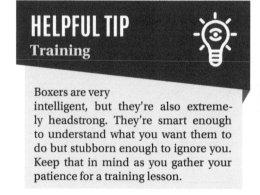

HELPFUL TIP
Training

Boxers are very intelligent, but they're also extremely headstrong. They're smart enough to understand what you want them to do but stubborn enough to ignore you. Keep that in mind as you gather your patience for a training lesson.

Absolutely. However, you may be doing too much at once. Train for short periods of time and stop when your dog is no longer receptive to training. Also, take a break if you find yourself getting so frustrated that you want to yell at your dog. Dogs can sense that kind of frustration and may become even more unruly. If practice is too daunting, try spending five to ten minutes a day working on the most important skills. Once you've mastered a few key commands, try another one. You may find that training becomes easier as your dog gets older and more mature. Eventually, your dog will get the hang of obedience training and it will be easier for both of you.

Half the battle of dog training is figuring out how dogs think—the other half is having the patience to work with an unpredictable animal. It's normal to get frustrated when your Boxer misbehaves or doesn't seem to be learning very quickly. However, dog training can be a lot of fun if you know the basics and have a positive attitude. Also, dog training can make life with a dog so much more pleasant because you have some control over an energetic animal. Once you understand the basic concepts, you'll be able to apply them to any command!

CHAPTER 10
Basic Commands

Most dog owners start obedience training with a few basic commands. Commands like shake and play dead are cute, but they do not serve a useful purpose when you're trying to get a dog under control. Save those tricks for later and focus on skills that you know will make life easier with your dog. For instance, if your Boxer tries to jump on anyone who approaches him, teaching him to sit may help him stay still when new people are around. Or, teaching your dog to stay can keep him out of harm's way when you can't physically restrain your Boxer. Here are a few useful commands that every dog (and dog owner) should know.

Photo Courtesy of Andrea Hicks

Sit

Start by teaching your boxer to focus on you. This helps him ignore other things that are going on around them. Then, teach the dog to sit. When I was teaching Zena to sit, I would hold the treat near her nose. After it got her attention, then I would slowly raise the treat up in the air. As her head came up, her butt went down until she reached the sitting position. Then, she got the treat. While she tried to jump a few times, she soon figured out that it was easier to comply and get the treat than jump and not get it. Soon, you can add the spoken command to sit. Some trainers, however, choose a word different than sit so that those who do not know the cue word will have a hard time getting the boxer to behave. While you can use almost any word, sit is "sentarse" in Spanish and "asseoir" in French. Because dogs don't speak human languages, you can use any cue word as long as you use it consistently.

Lie Down

Once your dog can sit, the next step is to teach him to lie down. Choose a cue word for this command and use that command consistently. Often times, people use "down" interchangeably when they want their dog to lie down and when they want their dog to get off of the furniture or jump down from someone's lap. So, try to use two different words for these very different actions.

With your Boxer in a seated position, hold the treat in front of his nose and slowly lower it to the floor, just in front of his paws. His head should follow the treat until his belly touches the floor. Once your dog is fully down say, "good down," and give him the treat. If your dog springs back up before you can say the command, do not give him the treat until he's fully on the ground.

Stay

Once your dog can sit and lie down, you'll want him to be able to hold that position until you release him. To teach this skill, start with your Boxer in the sitting position. Stand in front of your pup and hold your hand out in front of his face, as to say, "Stop." Give the "stay" command and slowly walk backwards a few steps. If your dog stays motionless for a few seconds, praise him and give him a treat. Each time you repeat this, add more time and distance in the sit or down position. For added difficulty, do this in a place with distractions.

When your dog has mastered this command, he'll stay put regardless of where you are and what's going on around you—until you release him

Photo Courtesy of Angie Alford

and call him to you. If your Boxer likes to bound out the door in front of you, practice sit and stay when you open the door. That way, your dog has to stay by your side and wait to go outside until you give him permission. When paired with sit or down, the stay command can give you a lot of control over a dog who's instinct tells him to get up and move.

Come

This is perhaps one of the most important commands to master with your Boxer. There will be times where your dog gets loose and panic starts to set in. Especially with active dogs who like to run and be chased, there's nothing more frightening than the thought of a loose dog that could get lost or run into traffic. But, if your dog can stop on a dime, turn around, and run straight to you with one word, you'll be able to help keep him from harm. The come command will get your Boxer to run straight towards you, no matter what else is going on.

This is where high value rewards come in handy. You want your Boxer to think that coming to you is the best thing in the whole world. So, get out your tastiest treats and best toys and show your dog what he can have if he does what you want. Start by having your dog sit and stay. Then, stand a few feet from your dog and say, "come." You can also add his name so you catch his attention before giving the command. Dogs tend to naturally go towards their owner, so if you act welcoming and show them a good reward, they'll likely come to right to you. Once your dog comes to you, give him the reward and tons of praise.

If your Boxer pup is reluctant to come straight to you, use his leash. Stand with a leash length of space between you and call your dog. If he doesn't run to you, give a gentle reminder tug on the leash. Then, make a big deal of your Boxer coming to you, even if you had to nudge him in your direction. Once your dog gets the hang of this command, create more distance and practice in places with more distractions. A 15 foot leash is good for practicing in distracting places because it allows you to get far away from your dog without putting him in a situation where he could easily run off. Plus, if your dog struggles with recall with larger distances, the long leash gives him the reminder he needs to come to you for his reward.

Off

Because Boxers are eager creatures that like to jump on people to say hello, you need a way to keep your dog from potentially hurting or scaring someone. For this command, wait until your dog naturally jumps on you. When this occurs, turn your back so that he has no reward. When all four feet are on the ground, say "good off" and reward him. Another way you can keep your dog from jumping on you is to put his leash on and drop the leash to the floor. Step on the leash so there is not enough length for your dog to jump up. When he tries to jump, he will get caught and will return to the ground. When he does, reward him for not jumping and let him know he did a good job jumping off.

Drop

Drop is a command that can be useful in various situations. A game of fetch is more successful if your dog drops the ball at your feet instead of holding onto it. There will also be moments when you catch your Boxer with something he shouldn't have in his mouth and you want him to let go of it immediately. If your dog has picked up something that is dangerous, this command can be life-saving. It's much easier to retrieve an item from your dog if he can drop it on command.

To teach this, give your dog a toy. Then, hold out a treat. Naturally, your dog will drop the item in order to eat the treat. Say "good drop" and give him the treat. After a few successful drops, give the drop command before you present the treat. Keep practicing until your Boxer drops the object every time, with or without a reward. Some dogs may be resistant to dropping their toy in exchange for a treat. Another way to reward the right behavior is to spend time with your dog and wait for him to drop a toy on his own accord. When this happens, give your dog praise for dropping the toy and give a treat.

Walk

Walking with a well-trained dog is a pleasure. Being yanked around by an unruly dog is a pain and will make it difficult to maintain your dog's exercise routine. Use good walking etiquette from the very start in order to avoid reinforcing bad habits.

Always walk with your Boxer on your left side. You don't want your dog to weave back and forth during a walk. Hold the leash with your left hand about halfway down the leash. This shortens the distance between you and your dog. His shoulder should roughly be in line with your hip, with him looking to you for direction. If he strays, give the leash a firm tug to correct his position. When he's back where he's supposed to be, give him tons of praise and a treat. You want to reinforce his position by your left leg, looking to you for direction.

Photo Courtesy of
Brynn Holic

Many dogs have the tendency to pull. I prefer to walk Zena with a harness because she was able to pull very hard even from the first day that I got her. When you use a harness, weight is evenly distributed across the dog's chest instead of him pulling and having all the pressure on his neck. I prefer a step-in harness because I find them easier to put on, but you can also use an over-the-head harness. Re-

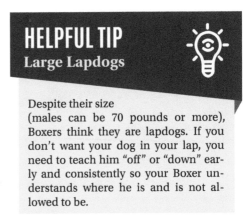

HELPFUL TIP
Large Lapdogs

Despite their size (males can be 70 pounds or more), Boxers think they are lapdogs. If you don't want your dog in your lap, you need to teach him "off" or "down" early and consistently so your Boxer understands where he is and is not allowed to be.

gardless, the best harnesses have wide straps and a cushioned chest strap.

In order to put on the harness, lay it on the floor so that it roughly resembles a figure eight on its side with one buckle coming off each side. Have the dog step into the harness. Then, bring the straps up around the Boxer's sides and snap the buckles together. You will not have to adjust the harness further until your Boxer grows.

A harness that clips on the back makes it easy for a dog to pull. That might work well for sled pulling, but not for walking. A harness that clips on the chest will make it hard for your dog to pull away from you. A pulling sensation around the collar will be unpleasant enough to deter your dog from pulling too much. Choke chains should be avoided because of the damage they can do to a dog's throat and neck.

Perhaps one of the most important things you can do when leash training your dog is to make sure he's not walking you when you should be walking him. If he pulls and does not take your corrections, make an abrupt about face so you're back in control. When your dog falls into line, give him praise and a treat. Be sure to pay close attention to your Boxer on walks so you can reward him every time he's walking nicely on the leash.

Once you're able to walk your dog with some slack in the leash, try new skills. You can teach him how to stop, go, speed up, and slow down on command. It's even possible to teach your dog how to turn left and right with a command! Once your dog is properly leash trained, you'll find yourself looking forward to your daily walks. Remember, dogs do not naturally know that they're supposed to walk alongside humans without stopping to sniff and chase everything. It will take some work before your dog is the perfect exercise companion.

Advanced Commands

Once your Boxer has mastered some of the most important commands, you can start working on some fun tricks. Don't stop training once your dog is proficient in basic skills—regular obedience training is great for your dog's brain and keeps him sharp. Plus, it's a lot of fun to show off how clever your dog is by performing tricks for your friends and family.

Shake/High Five

Shake is a great first trick because it's very easy to teach. To start, have your dog sit facing you. Put light pressure on the back of his leg, right above the paw so he naturally lifts that paw off of the ground. Once the paw is up, take it in your hand and give it a shake. Reward your dog and say, "shake." Keep practicing this until he raises his paw when you stick your hand out. If this method doesn't work, some owners find success in holding a treat in their hand and waiting for their dog to try to bat the treat away with their paw.

Once your Boxer is able to shake on command, try teaching high five. When teaching this trick, hold your hand up higher with an open palm in front of your dog's face, instead of a palm facing the ceiling, as you would for the shake command. If your dog doesn't automatically put his paw on your hand, hold it a little closer to his paw. As he starts to understand what you want, move your hand higher until you have a perfect high five!

Crawl

This is another fun activity that works your dog's mind and body. Start with your Boxer in the down position. Once his belly is touching the ground, hold a treat between his front paws. As he reaches for the treat, slowly drag it further away. He'll inch closer to the treat in order to get his prize. The further you move the treat, the further he'll scoot along the floor on his belly. However, if he gets on four legs to get the treat, have him lie back down and start over again. When he gets good at this trick, you can try to get him to crawl for long distances or even crawl underneath objects.

Sit Pretty

This trick is challenging, but can be very cute if your Boxer can learn it. To teach this, have your dog sit facing you. Take a treat and hold it just above your dog's nose, then slowly move it up and back. Your dog will follow the treat and in the process will slowly lift his front paws off of the ground. If your dog jumps up, you may be moving the treat too far and too fast. Reward your Boxer when he is sitting on his hind legs with his paws in front of him.

Don't be surprised if your Boxer is wobbly and tips over at first. Some dogs do not have the core strength needed for this trick and will have a hard time balancing. However, with lots of practice, your dog will get better at balancing and may one day be able to balance on his hind legs.

Spin

This trick will have your Boxer spinning in circles on cue. Start with your dog standing, facing you. Take a treat and make a slow circle with your hand. Start at your dog's nose and move either clockwise or counterclockwise. Your dog will follow your hand and turn in a circle. Practice turning in both directions, then eventually add the command "spin." In no time, your dog will be dancing around to your cues!

The number of commands you can teach your Boxer is endless. With training fundamentals and creativity, you can teach your dog how to perform all sorts of tasks! Make obedience training a regular part of your weekly routine to keep your dog active, well behaved, and entertained. You'll find that life with your Boxer is so much easier when you have more control over your dog and have established a mutual trust.

CHAPTER 11
Traveling With Your Boxer

Before long, you'll want to take your little buddy everywhere. Your Boxer is part of your family and it can be hard to spend time away from your fur babies. However, without the proper preparation, traveling with an animal can be difficult—both on you and your dog. In order to ensure everyone is safe and happy during your travels, here are some tips for leaving home when you have a Boxer.

Dog Carriers and Car Restraints

Photo Courtesy of Sabrina Harris

Dogs need to be restrained when riding in a car, both for the safety of your dog and your other passengers. Car rides can be exciting for a dog, and your Boxer might want to roam around the car or get your attention during a drive. This can be a huge distraction for a driver and can be very dangerous for your passengers or others on the road. Also, in the event of a crash or hard brake, your Boxer will go flying if he is not properly secured in the backseat. The last thing you want is for your Boxer to be injured in a car accident, so some sort of safety restraint is necessary for car travel.

There are different types of carriers and restraints to choose from. If your dog is crate trained, this is a great restraint for long trips. Your Boxer will feel safe and secure inside the rigid walls of the crate. In the event of a crash, your dog will be safe from flying debris and is less likely to have crushing injuries.

For shorter trips and for dogs that are not comfortable with crates, a seatbelt and harness system is easy and affordable. Dog seatbelts can be purchased at a pet store. These are simple straps with one end that clicks into a car's seatbelt and the other end attaches to your dog's collar or harness like a leash. You can use a collar to keep your dog in the backseat during a drive, but you may want to use a harness for safety reasons. This is because in the event of a crash, a harness will distribute your dog's body weight throughout his muscular shoulders and chest, as opposed to a collar, which places stress on a thin band around your dog's sensitive neck.

Photo Courtesy of
Stephanie DesEnfants

Photo Courtesy of Jerri Ruiz

There are soft carrier bags on the market that will keep a dog comfortable and secure during a car ride, but these are typically geared towards small dogs. You may enjoy the ease of a carrier bag, but only during the puppy days when your Boxer is portable! There are also seat protectors on the market that hook onto your car's headrests to make a hammock between the front and back seats, which can help prevent your dog from flying forward in a crash. As an added bonus, seat protectors will keep your car seats clean. Whatever you choose to keep you and your dog safe in your vehicle, make sure it is the appropriate size for your Boxer and will keep him safely restrained in the backseat.

Preparing Your Dog for Car Rides

Some dogs love car rides while others tremble at the thought of getting in a car. It's hard to know how your Boxer will react until you need to take him somewhere for the first time. In order to start your trip off on the right foot, you'll want to get your dog used to being in a moving vehicle. Like with any kind of dog training, you can do this through positive reinforcement.

First, let your dog jump in your car and give him a treat. Sit in the car with your dog for a little while and give him treats and pets. When your dog is comfortable sitting in your car, buckle him in and take the car for a drive around the block. If your dog remains calm during this time, give him a treat. It can be helpful to have a human passenger in your car to talk to your pup in a soothing voice while giving out treats. As your Boxer becomes more comfortable in your car, go on increasingly longer drives until he is calm and comfortable going for a ride. Ideally, your dog will enjoy this time with you so much that he'll jump in the backseat on command.

Some dogs experience car sickness, which can make rides very unpleasant. In most car sickness cases, the dog gets nauseated because he is nervous to begin with, and the motion of the car doesn't make him feel any better. If your Boxer gets carsick, you may need to practice sitting in the car with positive reinforcement. Or, talk to your vet about medications you can give your dog if you absolutely need to go for a ride.

Flying and Hotel Stays

Flying with a Boxer can be complicated. Oftentimes, airlines do not allow larger dogs to fly in the cabin and require canine passengers to ride in the cargo hold. While dogs commonly go on flights, it's important to be aware of what air travel can be like for a dog. Your dog will ride in a dark, noisy compartment, and the temperature isn't as well-regulated as it is in the cabin. Plus, the change in air pressure can be uncomfortable to a dog that has never experienced it before. Not to mention, your dog will be separated from you during this confusing and potentially scary time. There are times where air travel with your Boxer may be unavoidable, but consider what your dog will experience before taking him on nonessential flights.

If your dog must fly, make sure that both your dog and your crate have ample identification. Your Boxer should be wearing a collar tag with your contact information, plus a microchip in case the collar tag falls off. It's also a good idea to have your contact information written on your dog's crate.

HELPFUL TIP
Hotel Rules

While more hotels are becoming dog-friendly, many hotels have size limits, and some have breed restrictions. Since Boxers are often considered a "bully breed," be sure to call any hotel where you hope to take your Boxer and find out the rules before you make a reservation. You don't want to show up at your hotel and be turned away just because you have a Boxer.

Put a favorite blanket and comforting toy in the crate, along with some water. Keep the airline and airport's contact information on hand, just in case your dog is not transferred to the right location after the flight. Locate the dog walk areas in airports and allow your Boxer plenty of time to go to the bathroom and stretch his legs before getting on the plane.

Once you get to your destination, you will want some time to unwind with your pup. When choosing a hotel, ensure that you've picked one that allows dogs. It can be a headache to get to your hotel and either be turned away or fined for bringing your Boxer. If the hotel listing doesn't explicitly state that larger dogs are allowed, double check before booking. Also, your hotel may be dog-friendly, but the area may not be. Look for a place that has a nearby park or somewhere you feel safe walking around. Your Boxer will not be happy if he has to sit in a small room all day when he's probably already feeling nervous and excited about being in a new place. It's helpful to keep as much of your normal routine as you can.

Because you don't want your Boxer to tear up a rented room, it's important to give him the exercise he needs, especially if you will not be with him the entirety of your stay. Go on a long walk around the place you're visiting or find a local dog park to play a long game of fetch. Get him nice and tired before going back to the room. Also, make sure you have his favorite blanket or a favorite toy on hand to soothe him in this unfamiliar place. This can also be a good opportunity to break out a new puzzle toy to keep him busy.

Kenneling vs. Dog Sitters

Sometimes, it's best to leave your Boxer at home when you have to travel. If you're going on a trip and know that you may be putting your dog under stress to take him along, make other plans for him. It might be nice to have a travel partner when going on a business trip, but if you're spending long days in meetings while your dog waits in a hotel room, he may have a better time at home.

What you do with your Boxer depends on your dog's personality. If your dog is super friendly, plays well with others, and can handle a lot of commotion, a kennel will work well for your Boxer. These are boarding facilities that house many dogs at once. The benefits of a kennel include lots of human supervision and plenty of opportunities to play and socialize with other dogs. These facilities also tend to be more affordable because the employees are looking after several dogs at once.

If your dog is shy around others, can be overwhelmed by lots of barking, or generally does not do well in social situations, it might be better to hire a sitter. This is someone who either watches your Boxer at their house, or will come to your house to care for your dog. This option is nice because your dog can stay in a familiar place and won't be overwhelmed by other dogs or people. If you hire a dog sitter, have the sitter visit before you leave to let your Boxer become comfortable with the stranger. Private sitters can be more expensive because they are only looking after one dog, but if you know your dog will not be happy at a kennel, a sitter is the right choice.

Photo Courtesy of
Olivia Salgado

Tips and Tricks for Traveling

Photo Courtesy of Lori Scherer

Before you leave for your trip, make a packing list for your dog. Include dishes, food, treats, a few favorite toys, extra poop bags, a harness, and a leash. Fill a reusable water bottle that can easily be emptied into a dish in your car. If you plan to take frequent trips with your Boxer, it helps to have a designated dog bag that you can pull out of the closet and fill with the essentials when you're about to hit the road.

On a long car trip, make strategic stops along the way so your dog doesn't have to go to the bathroom in an alley by a gas station. Map out a few parks or grassy rest stops along the way so you can walk around for a few minutes before getting back in the car. Be aware that if your Boxer is accustomed to going to the bathroom on grass, expecting him to potty on a concrete sidewalk may be difficult. As long as your stops are safe, let your dog out to sniff around every time you stop. But, if you're in an area with lots of traffic, it might be best to keep your dog restrained until you can get to a place with more space to walk around.

If you're worried about your dog's behavior or anxiety during a trip, one of the best things you can do is make sure your dog has ample exercise. A tired dog is a relaxed dog. Before you leave on your trip, take your dog on a long walk or a quick jog. If you're staying in a hotel and will have to be away from your Boxer for any length of time, find a place for your dog to run around until he's exhausted, or fill a puzzle toy with treats before you head out. Travel can be tough on a dog, but if you take the time to make sure your little buddy gets his physical and mental exercise needs met, it will be easier on both of you.

Finally, make sure your Boxer always has some form of identification on him at all times. Have your dog wear his collar with updated information at all times. In the event that your dog gets loose and isn't wearing his collar, a microchip can reunite you with your dog if he is picked up and brought to a facility with a chip reader. Even if your Boxer walks off-leash at home, avoid ever letting your dog loose in an unfamiliar place. The last thing you want to do on your trip is to search for your missing dog.

Boxers can make excellent travel companions. In order to maximize your fun on your trip, it's important to ensure that your dog's needs are met. Only take your dog on a trip if you know that it won't cause him undue stress. If you're leaving your pup at home, choose accommodations that will make your dog comfortable while you're away. With some extra planning and thinking ahead, you'll find that travels with your furry friend can be a lot of fun. After all, part of the fun of having a Boxer is letting him meet new people and smell new things!

CHAPTER 12
Nutrition

"Boxer tend to have a fair amount of food allergies, they also are prone to bloat. Make sure you choose a food with a good high quality protein source, avoid fillers especially low quality like corn and barley. My dogs do best on Salmon or Venison. Don't let them eat their food quickly and try to elevate their bowls off the floor a little if possible."

Melissa Looman
Country Hill Boxers

Your Boxer's nutrition is an important part of his overall health and wellbeing. Unlike humans, who eat a wide variety of foods in their daily diets, dogs tend to eat the same kibble and treats on a daily basis. When choosing a food, it's important to find a formula that gives your Boxer the nutrients he needs to be healthy and live a long life. This chapter will discuss what your dog needs in his diet and how to ensure he gets the necessary nutrients.

Photo Courtesy of
Zoe Brewster

Importance of Good Diet

Without the right food, your Boxer will not be at peak performance. Even if your dog isn't competing in sports, you want him to be full of energy, healthy, and feel good. If your dog's food isn't right for him, he could be fatigued, ill, or suffer from allergies. If your Boxer's favorite thing to do is go on long walks, but his food is not giving him the lasting energy he needs to sustain his exercise, it's going to hurt his overall happiness. If your dog is allergic to an ingredient in his dog food or it doesn't have enough fat, your pup could end up feeling very itchy and uncomfortable. If the formula doesn't have the right nutrients, your senior dog could have joint pain and have trouble climbing onto the couch with you. What your Boxer eats can have a big impact on his health and happiness his entire life.

A healthy balance of all essential nutrients is key. A good dog food should have a mix of carbohydrates from different sources, and should contain some whole grain ingredients. Corn, wheat, and soy are common in dog food, but a mix of brown rice, barley, and oatmeal can give your dog some long lasting energy and is easy for dogs to digest. Protein is a necessary part of a Boxer's diet and can come in various animal sources. Red meats are full of iron, chicken is a lean source of protein, and fish contains good fatty acids that are great for a dog's overall health. These keep your dog's skin moisturized and give him a shiny coat.

While fruits and vegetables provide a natural source of vitamins and minerals, most commercial dog foods contain vitamin and mineral supplements so your dog gets all of the nutrients he needs. Many formulas also contain antioxidants, fiber, and supplements that keep your dog's joints healthy.

When choosing a dog food, ask your breeder or vet for their recommendation. A reputable, experienced Boxer breeder will likely have a preferred brand of dog food that has proven to keep his or her dogs healthy. A vet will also be the first person to know if a certain brand or type of dog food is not a good pick. For example, after studies came out that suggested grain free diets led to heart disease in dogs, my vet made sure my dog's food contained grains. Also, keep your budget in mind when choosing a dog food. Some dog foods come at a high price, which can be hard to buy month after month. On the other hand, some dog foods are cheap because they do not contain high quality ingredients. When shopping for a dog food, pick a formula that is in the middle of the extreme prices. That way, your dog gets quality nutrition without breaking the bank.

The Role of Protein in Your Boxer's Diet

Boxers, and other muscular dog breeds, need a little extra protein in their diet. Without protein, your dog might not be able to put on enough muscle to do the activities he loves to do. A general adult formula may not have enough protein for a very active Boxer. There are specialty dog foods on the market that cater to specific breeds and have a mix of proteins, fats, and carbs that best suit a muscular dog's body.

Plant-based diets in humans have become popular in recent years, but are not appropriate for a dog. Dogs can get protein from plant sources, but their food should also contain meat. Meat contains a more complete source of necessary amino acids and other beneficial nutrients that keeps his body healthy. There are many valid reasons why a person may choose not to eat animal products, but a dog does not get a say in the type of dog food he eats. Regardless of your opinions on eating animals, make sure your dog gets protein, fat, and other nutrients from a meat-based diet.

Photo Courtesy of
Jennifer Bentley

Wet Vs. Dry Dog Food

"When you first bring your boxer home watch their stools, if they are super runny have your vet check them out. Switching from the brand of dog food that the breeder used to the brand that the new owners want to use needs to be a slow transition. Otherwise it is hard on their digestive system."

Brad & Gail Quistorff
Breezy Boxers

Both wet and dry dog foods have their pros and cons, so consider which is best for your dog. Wet foods contain lots of moisture, which makes the food very aromatic and appealing for a dog. If your Boxer is extremely picky and turns his nose up at dry food, you may want to try mixing a portion of wet food with the dry. Also, wet food is good for dogs who have trouble eating crunchy kibble, either due to dental disease or mouth disfigurations. On the other hand, wet food sticks to teeth, which can lead to a higher rate of decay.

Dry food can be beneficial to your dog's oral hygiene because the hard surface scrapes plaque off of his teeth as your dog chews. This will save you a lot of time and money in the future if your dog does not require as many professional teeth cleanings. Also, many owners find it more convenient to buy dry food in bulk, as opposed to a bunch of heavy cans. As long as there are no issues that prevent your Boxer from eating dry food, many consider it the better option.

HELPFUL TIP
Weight Management

Maintaining a Boxer's ideal weight can be a bit of a chore. While they are prone to obesity as much as other dog breeds, they can also be underweight if you don't feed them enough for their energy level. You should be able to feel, but not see, your Boxer's ribs. He should have a defined, but not extreme, waistline. If you aren't sure whether your Boxer is a healthy weight, be sure to talk to your vet, since being over- or underweight can cause health problems.

Cooking for Your Boxer

Some owners choose to forgo the dog food selection process and make their own dog food! This can be a nutritious way to ensure that you know everything that goes into your Boxer's diet. However, be prepared to spend more time and money making your dog's meals than you would if you gave your pup a few scoops of dry food a day. You'll need to buy fresh meats and produce at least once a week to ensure nothing goes rancid.

Chicken, fish, and organ meats are good sources of protein and fats that your dog will enjoy. Steamed fruits and veggies give your dog essential vitamins and minerals. Potatoes, rice, barley, and sweet potatoes provide plenty of energy for your dog to play all day. Some dog owners also add multivitamin supplements to a homemade diet to make sure no necessary nutrient is missing.

If you decide that you want to make your Boxer's meals, consult with a veterinarian before proceeding. Many well intentioned dog owners fall short of their dog's nutritional needs because they do not have the required knowledge it takes to make dog food. A veterinarian can tell you what your Boxer needs to be healthy.

Feeding Table Scraps

It's hard to resist your Boxer's puppy eyes when he spots the fat trimmings from your steak and you don't want to let food go to waste, but oftentimes you're doing your dog a disservice by letting him clean your plate. Feeding your dog table scraps can be harmful because you may accidentally feed him something that will make him sick, it can add unnecessary calories to his already balanced diet, and it can reinforce annoying begging behaviors.

When you give your Boxer leftovers, you may forget the ingredients that went into your meal. Onions, for example, are found in lots of human meals, but are not good for dogs. Packaged food contains salt, artificial sweeteners, and preservatives you may not realize are included in your food. Foods with dairy may be hard on your Boxer's stomach if he's not used to eating them, resulting in diarrhea and gas. You can make your dog ill by letting him lick your plate clean.

Table scraps are also not accounted for in your dog's daily diet. Dog food servings are calculated by your dog's weight, so he gets approximately as many calories as he needs to maintain a healthy weight. Unless you ad-

Photo Courtesy of
Wendy Isbill

just your Boxer's meals to include calories from excessive treats and supplementary foods, giving him table scraps can lead to weight gain which can result in a whole host of health problems.

Finally, feeding your dog table scraps can create bad habits. If you like to drop food from your plate to your dog during a meal, this tells your dog that he will be rewarded if he hangs around close during dinner. Similarly, if he knows you will dump your plate in his dish after a meal, he might whine while you eat because he is getting impatient for his treat. He may even pester your dinner guests for their food. This habit can be hard to break, so it's important that your dog does not make a connection between your meal time and a special treat. If you choose to feed your Boxer leftovers, it may be best to hold them to the side while you do dishes and clean up the kitchen before dumping the food in his dish. That way, he is less likely to beg while you eat.

Feeding dogs "people food" can be beneficial if the right foods are selected and given at the right time. The foods we eat can be healthy training treats for a dog. Instead of rewarding your pup with a commercial dog treat after completing a command, try giving him a blueberry or a small chunk of steamed (and cooled) sweet potato. He may find this novelty treat motivating and you'll know that it's good for his health.

Treats

Treats are part of every dog's diet and should be chosen carefully, just like your dog's food. Because treats are primarily used for training purposes, it's important to find ones that make your Boxer go wild. Otherwise, he won't be motivated to learn. Choose a dog treat that gives off a strong scent because it will catch your Boxer's attention. Also, choose a treat that is easy to break into small pieces. If you use a large biscuit as a reward, it will take your dog a long time to eat it and derail the training. Jerky strips or sticks can easily be torn into small pieces and contain the moisture that gives off meaty scents. Or, you can buy treats already designed for training purposes that are small and can be eaten quickly. As mentioned earlier, fruits and vegetables can also be used as a healthy dog treat alternative and high-stakes treats like hot dogs can be used on special occasions when you really need your Boxer to focus. Avoid overfeeding treats because it makes the treats less motivating for training and can cause weight gain.

Weight Management

When dogs eat more calories than they burn, they are liable to gain weight. Over time, too much weight can be very hard on your dog's body. Extra weight puts a lot of stress on bones and joints, leading to injuries. Extra fat can also line organs, making your dog's body work harder, just to carry out normal function. An overweight dog may also have a hard time doing the activities he once loved, like running and jumping.

Male Boxers tend to weigh between 60-80 pounds and females are a little smaller at 50-65 pounds. If you suspect your pup is getting a little too chunky, many pet stores with vet clinics have scales you're welcome to use. Another way you can tell if your Boxer is at a healthy weight is by looking at him from the top. If his body is wide at the shoulders, then dips in at the hips, he's likely at a healthy weight. If his body is completely straight at the sides, he's probably carrying some extra fat. You can also do a feel test. Run your hands along your dog's ribs—if you can feel his ribs, but they are not visible through the skin, he's probably at a healthy weight. A vet will always tell you if your dog's weight is healthy during a checkup.

If your dog is overweight, first talk to your vet about working on a plan to get your Boxer back into shape. Keep a close eye on everything your dog eats during the day. If your dog eats your leftovers frequently, cut that from his daily diet. If you give your dog a lot of training treats, break them into smaller pieces, find lower calorie treats, or reduce the number of treat rewards you give. Also, make sure you are giving your Boxer the recommended amount of food according to the dog food bag, and not topping off the cup to please your pup.

Along with reducing the amount of calories, you'll also need to make sure your Boxer is getting the exercise he needs to shed pounds. Exercise can be hard on an overweight dog's body, so start slow and build his endurance. It might be too much to start with him running a few miles a day, so start with a gentle walk or swim. In time, you'll be able to run and play with your Boxer without him getting overly exhausted or injured. Until then, take it easy and watch for signs of exhaustion or heat-related illness.

Your dog's diet can have a big impact on the length and quality of life he lives. Good food can keep your Boxer energized and feeling good. The right nutrients can even keep your dog's coat shiny and eyes bright. Dogs need a balance of calories and physical activity to stay healthy, so be mindful of your pup's food intake and daily exercise. Most commercial dog foods and treats will work well for Boxers, but always check with a veterinarian if you're concerned about your dog's nutrition.

CHAPTER 13
Grooming Your Boxer

Grooming isn't just for show dogs! A regular grooming routine will not only keep your Boxer looking good, but will also keep him healthy. Grooming can be done by a professional, but it can also easily be done at home for a fraction of the price. This chapter will tell you what types of grooming your Boxer needs and how to carry out these steps.

Coat Basics

The Boxer has a very low maintenance coat. The short hairs of their coat make these dogs easy to brush and clean. While other long haired dogs may need a full bath after they get dirty, your Boxer can be cleaned up with a quick wipe! Because this breed has straight fur, you can expect your Boxer to shed. However, frequent brushing with a natural bristled brush can distribute healthy oils and keep loose hairs from flying all over your home. Your Boxer's fur will never tangle, but regular brushing is necessary to keep his skin and fur properly moisturized and clean.

HELPFUL TIP
Shedding

For as short as their hair is, you may be surprised at how much Boxers can shed, and their splinter-like hair can embed itself in your clothing and furniture. Reduce the amount of hair around your home by giving your pet a vigorous brushing once or twice a week with a rubber, curry-style brush (like a Zoom Groom) or a bristle brush to remove loose hair before it falls all over your home.

Bath Time

On rare occasions, your Boxer will need a bath. Because frequent bathing can strip your dog's coat and skin of necessary oils, try to limit bath time to when your pup is especially dirty or smelly, such as when he rolls in something smelly or jumps in a mud puddle. Aside from such incidents, four to six baths a year is all your dog needs.

Some dogs do not like baths, so give your Boxer some positive reinforcement when you bathe him. Most owners put their dog in the tub, but a garden hose or a baby pool will also work well. Or, some pet stores and doggy daycares have facilities where you can groom your own dog. Have plenty of treats on hand to give during the bath. Make sure that the water isn't too hot or too cold. Wet your dog by gently pouring a cup of water on his body or by using a gentle setting on a handheld showerhead. Keep water away from the face because soap and water in the ears and eyes can be very uncomfortable. When it's time to wash your dog's face, use a damp cloth to carefully wipe around the ears and eyes. When it comes to shampoo, it's best to use a gentle formula

Photo Courtesy of Linda Meeks

that won't be too drying or fragrant. Some dogs are susceptible to allergies and skin irritations, so a gentle, sensitive-skin formula should work well with your Boxer. Also, never use human shampoo on your dog, as it could irritate your dog's skin.

After shampooing, make sure you rinse your dog thoroughly as shampoo residue will make your dog's skin feel dry and itchy. Once you think you've rinsed off all of the shampoo, give your dog one last rinse, just to be sure the soap is really gone. Pat your dog dry with a towel, and you're good to go!

Time for a Pedicure

Dogs have sharp claws that can scratch you and your belongings if they aren't kept at a reasonable length. Furthermore, if nails grow too long, the length will put excess pressure on your Boxer's paws. Over time, walking around on overgrown nails will lead to skeletal problems that can cause pain and lameness.

Some dogs do not like the sensation of having their nails cut, so before you start trimming, get your dog used to the trimmers. Hold the clippers next to your Boxer's foot and give him a treat and some praise. You can also hold your dog's paw and touch his toenails, giving him a treat when he sits still. Once he can tolerate someone touching his toenails and feel calm when there's a strange contraption near his feet, he'll be ready to have his nails clipped.

When cutting the toenails, be careful not to cut too far and damage the quick, or blood supply, to the nail. This can be very painful and make your

Boxer even more resistant to having his nails trimmed. If you do happen to nick the blood vessel, use styptic powder and apply pressure to the area until the bleeding stops. If your Boxer has clear nails, you'll be able to see the pink quick in the nail, making it easy to avoid. If your dog has black nails, this task can be tricky, so try to snip small segments until the nail no longer touches the ground when your Boxer is standing.

If your dog hates nail clippers, you may want to try a nail grinder instead. This is a device that gently sands your dog's toenails down to a dull surface. But, if you don't want to spend money on a device your dog will run from, you may want to take your Boxer to the groomer and see if he tolerates it before buying a nail grinder of your own.

Brushing Teeth

Regular tooth brushing not only keeps bad breath at bay, but it can also enhance your dog's health. When nasty plaque and bacteria build up on dog teeth, this can ultimately work its way into the blood system, causing infection in important organs, like the heart. Over time, a dog's dirty teeth can lead to serious tooth decay and tooth loss, making it difficult or painful to eat. A vet can provide professional cleanings, but these can be expensive and require your Boxer to go under sedation, which can be hard on older dogs. One of the best things you can do for your dog's health is brush his teeth on a regular basis.

First, buy a toothbrush that fits your Boxer's mouth. Human toothbrushes are too big, so purchase a dog toothbrush at a pet store, or use a child's toothbrush. You will need toothpaste that has been designed specifically for canine use because dogs are unable to spit out toothpaste. Dog toothpastes tend to come in dog-friendly flavors like chicken and peanut butter, and contain enzymes that clean teeth.

To start, put some toothpaste on your finger and let your Boxer lick it off. Usually, dogs like the flavors in these pastes and might see it as a tasty treat. Next, put a little paste on the toothbrush and let your dog lick it off. Finally, lift your dog's lip and start gently brushing the outer surface of the tooth. This is the dirtiest part of the tooth, as crunchy food does a good job of scraping plaque off the inside surface.

In addition to daily brushing, playing with a rope toy will also scrape some plaque from your dog's teeth. Some treats claim to have dental benefits and are mint-flavored to keep your dog's breath fresh between brushings. Chewing is good for your dog's dental hygiene, so always have chew toys available.

Cleaning Ears and Eyes

Ears and eyes are delicate parts of your dog's body that also need special attention. A dog's ears will naturally produce wax to protect the ear. However, too much dirt or wax buildup can make your dog's ears feel itchy or uncomfortable. To clean your Boxers ears, squirt an ear cleaning solution in the ear and massage the ear. This can be pur-

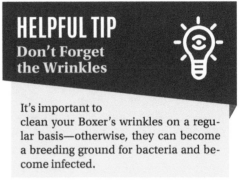

HELPFUL TIP

Don't Forget the Wrinkles

It's important to clean your Boxer's wrinkles on a regular basis—otherwise, they can become a breeding ground for bacteria and become infected.

chased at a pet store or veterinary clinic. Once you massage the solution into your Boxer's ears, he'll shake his head to displace the moisture, causing excess wax to come out. You can wipe the outer parts of the ear with a damp cloth, but avoid clean the inner ear, where the sensitive eardrum is located. Clean your dog's ears whenever there is a lot of wax buildup, your dog is scratching at his ears a lot, or if they appear irritated. If cleaning doesn't fix the problem, take your pooch to the vet—he may need to be treated for an infection.

Eyes may also need special attention from time to time. If your Boxer has a white face, the goop around the corners of his eyes may cause staining. This doesn't hurt the dog, but it looks unsightly. Tear stains can be cleaned with a solution you can buy at pet stores. Otherwise, gently wipe the corners of your dog's eyes with a damp cloth to remove any dirt and debris. If your Boxer's eyes are especially red, watery, oozing, or are causing your dog discomfort, see a vet immediately.

Keeping up with your dog's hygiene will not only make him look good, but he'll feel so much better too! These are all tasks that can be done at home, or you can take your dog to a groomer to help you keep your Boxer looking fresh. The downfall of using a groomer is that you'll have to include regular grooming in your budget, but for some dog owners, this is worth it. If your dog is too squirmy to cut his nails and you're afraid of nicking the quick, $20 every few months is a small expense to keep your dog's nails trimmed. Or, if your shower makes bathing your dog a mess, you can always drop your pup off at the groomer for a full makeover a few times a year. While it's cheaper and more convenient to take care of grooming at home, it's best to take to your dog to a groomer if there's any reason why you're unable to carry out these tasks at home. Grooming is essential to your Boxer's overall health and happiness.

CHAPTER 14
Basic Health Care

There's nothing more important than your dog's health. Every Boxer owner wants their best friend to live as long as possible. Good preventive healthcare will improve your dog's quality of life and help him grow into a senior dog. Along with regular vet visits, you will need to watch out for some common ailments in dogs so your Boxer will have a healthy life. This chapter will outline some basic canine healthcare information that you'll want to keep in mind while you raise your Boxer.

Photo Courtesy of
Erin Benner

Photo Courtesy of Patricia Densten

Fleas and Ticks

Fleas and ticks are nasty external parasites that latch onto your Boxer and suck his blood. These pests hitch a ride on your dog after he's been playing in the grass or hanging out with other animals. These parasites can carry disease and cause anemia if too much blood has been lost. However, these parasites can be repelled by a monthly topical or oral medication that is prescribed by a veterinarian.

If your dog returns from his adventures outside with ticks stuck to his skin, be careful when removing them. Make sure to grasp the tick near the head and gently pull the whole tick off. Otherwise, you risk ripping the tick's body and leaving the head attached to your dog's skin. If you live in an area with ticks, be sure to check your dog over before bringing him inside. Especially if your dog likes to cuddle with people, these ticks can detach and find a human source of blood.

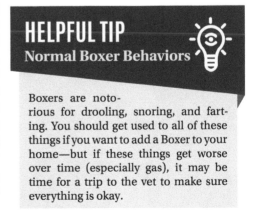

HELPFUL TIP
Normal Boxer Behaviors

Boxers are notorious for drooling, snoring, and farting. You should get used to all of these things if you want to add a Boxer to your home—but if these things get worse over time (especially gas), it may be time for a trip to the vet to make sure everything is okay.

Photo Courtesy of Sandra Martin

Fleas can be a nightmare if your Boxer becomes infested because of how quickly they reproduce and how easily they jump from place to place. If your dog has fleas, immediately bathe him in flea shampoo and comb through his fur with a flea comb, crushing any insect you find in his fur. Then, you'll have to thoroughly clean your home. Wash all bedding that your dog has contact with in hot water and vacuum every surface of your home. Fleas can lay eggs in the tiny cracks in your floorboards or nooks in your couch and return in no time. Purchase a flea-killing cleaning spray that will kill eggs, or use a bug bomb in affected areas. With enough diligence, you'll be able to rid your dog and home of fleas. If your current flea prevention isn't working, see your vet about a more effective preventative treatment. Avoid flea collars, especially if you own cats, because they can be lethal to felines and are a possible carcinogen to dogs.

Worms and Internal Parasites

Internal parasites are other nasty creatures that can make your dog very ill. When worms are feeding on your dog that means your dog isn't getting the nutrients he needs to be healthy. Intestinal worms are somewhat common in dogs—especially puppies. If you find worms in your dog's stool, your vet will want a sample so he can prescribe the proper medication. These infestations tend to clear up in no time. If you notice that your Boxer is looking lethargic, has abnormal bowel movements, or appears generally under the weather, you may need to collect a sample for your vet to analyze. Hookworms, whipworms, tapeworms, and roundworms are common types of intestinal worms, but only roundworms and tapeworms can be seen with the naked eye. So, if your dog displays any stomach issues that don't clear up after a few hours, you will need to prepare a stool sample to take to your vet. Fortunately, de-worming medication can help your dog feel better in no time.

Heartworms are another parasite that feeds off of a dog's insides, but this can be deadly if not caught in time. When a dog is bitten by a mosquito that carries the parasite, the worms enter the body through the bloodstream and grow into the dog's heart. It is treatable when caught early, but can cause serious illness and death if treated too late. Fortunately, your dog can take a preventative pill each month to protect him from this dangerous parasite. Your vet will likely test your dog's blood on a yearly basis as he prescribes a six month or yearlong supply of the preventative medicine.

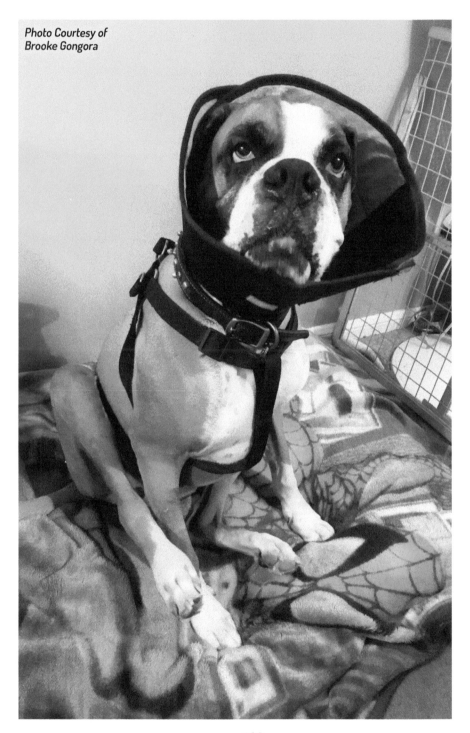

Photo Courtesy of
Brooke Gongora

Natural Health Care and Your Boxer

Some dog owners like to use "natural" methods of keeping their dog healthy. There may be some herbs and naturally occurring ingredients that could boost your dog's health. For example, glucosamine, which is found in animal cartilage, is believed to be excellent for joint health in dogs. Some herbal supplements on the market may help calm an anxious dog during thunderstorms or car rides. When considering non-pharmaceutical remedies, consult with a veterinarian first. "Natural" doesn't always mean healthy, and consumers are often lulled into a false sense of safety because natural remedies seem harmless. Not only can some "natural" remedies be harmful, but they are often given in place of life saving pharmaceuticals that can improve a dog's life. Supplements may improve your dog's health and give him a shiny coat, but they should not replace medicine prescribed by a vet.

Vaccinations

When you visit the vet for your Boxer's yearly checkup, your vet will make sure your pup is up to date on his shots. Some vaccines are legally required, like rabies, but others are the owner's choice. While vaccines are an added cost, they are necessary to your dog's good health. Not only that, but the more dogs that are vaccinated, the harder it is for a virus to spread, which could save the lives of many dogs. Also, the cost of a vaccine pales in comparison to the stress a preventable illness puts on you and your dog.

If you visit the same vet office for every checkup, you won't need to worry about what shots your dog has had because their office will keep a detailed list of vaccine records. If you switch clinics, they'll make sure you have your dog's records available to take to the new vet. For starters, your dog will need shots for rabies, DHPP, and Bordetella. However, there are other regionally-based viruses, like Rocky Mountain Spotted Fever, that may require a different vaccine. As always, make sure you listen to your vet's vaccination recommendations. Also, many trainers and boarding facilities require any dogs in their building to have records of their shots before they can enter.

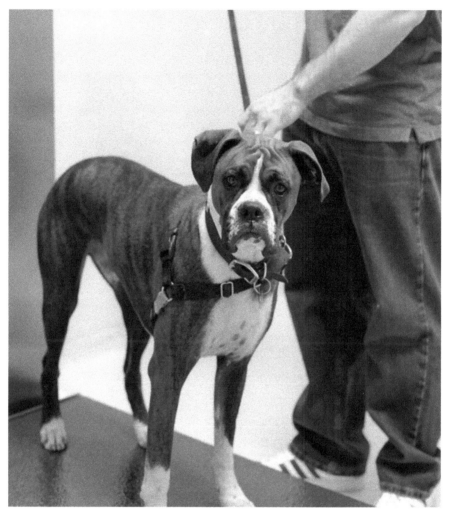

Pet Insurance

Health insurance is not only for humans—your dog can also benefit from an insurance policy. Many veterinary clinics, especially larger chains, offer different kinds of health plans that can make veterinary care more affordable. You can also purchase pet insurance through a major insurance carrier. There are also different types of policies to choose from. Some will cover basic preventative care, like your pup's regular checkups, while other plans will cover illness, injury, or chronic conditions. You will likely have to pay the full vet bill upfront after a visit, but you will be reimbursed by your insurance carrier after filing a claim.

If your Boxer lives a healthy life with few health problems, your monthly premiums will likely exceed what you would have otherwise paid in vet bills. However, if your Boxer unexpectedly becomes sick or injured, pet insurance can save you money in the long run. If you want to make sure that you have plenty of funds to take care of your Boxer and don't want to pay insurance for an otherwise healthy pooch, you can always set aside money every month for your dog's healthcare needs.

Preventative care is best when it comes to ensuring your Boxer has a long and healthy life. Shortly after you bring your puppy home, establish a regular veterinarian and start your dog on his necessary vaccinations. When you visit the vet, have him write a prescription for parasite prevention drugs so no creature can feast on your Boxer. Finally, be sure to maintain your yearly appointments at the vet so any health concern can be discussed before becoming too serious. When you're in doubt about your dog's health, it's best to talk to the experts as soon as possible.

CHAPTER 15

Advanced Boxer Health and Your Aging Boxer

Sometimes, your dog's health is more complicated than remember-ing to go to the vet for a checkup once a year. Every breed has a few genetic diseases that are more common in that breed than others. And, though we try to prevent illness and injury, accidents happen. Even-tually, our dogs become seniors and need a little special attention. While the thought of a sick Boxer can be frightening, it's important to be pre-pared for anything so you'll quickly be able to recognize when your dog needs extra care.

Photo Courtesy of
James Varughese

Boxer First Aid Basics

It would be great if you never experienced an emergency with your Boxer, but that is unrealistic. Therefore, you need to make sure that you are prepared for emergencies and have a basic idea of what to do before you can get your dog to the vet. While I can call my vet any time of the day or night and someone will return my phone call in about 10 minutes, I still need to have the supplies on hand to do basic first aid should Zena need it.

It is natural for your Boxer to be scared when injured. Therefore, he may try to snap, scratch, or bite you. While you may just have to tolerate the scratches, muzzling your Boxer can help stop the biting. That is why you should teach your dog to wear one before it is needed. That said, you should, never muzzle a Boxer who is vomiting.

When possible, stabilize any injuries before trying to move your pet. You should have a pet first aid kit that you take with you everywhere that your Boxer goes. The kit should include plenty of bandages and splints of different sizes that you can use in an emergency. Talk to your vet about how to stabilize injuries because there is nothing like a hands-on demonstration for learning. Hydrogen peroxide can be used to induce vomiting if your dog eats something dangerous. Keep tweezers on hand to remove splinters, thorns, and sand burrs. Antibiotic ointment and alcohol swabs can clean a small wound in a pinch. It's also helpful to keep styptic powder on hand to stop bleeding, especially if you cut your dog's toenails. Or, instead of making your own first aid kit, you can buy one from a pet store or sporting goods store.

Your pet should be moved to the vet in a small cage. If that is not available quickly, then use a cardboard box. Try to keep the Boxer confined in a small space. Be careful, however, that you do not put your face in the dog's face or try to hug your Boxer. He's hurting right now and trying to comfort him is a natural instinct, however, an injured pet can act irrationally doing things it would normally not do, like try to bite you.

Seek professional help as quickly as possible. Just like minutes often count in human emergencies, they count in Boxer emergencies too. If possible, talk to your vet on the phone and follow his advice. If your regular vet clinic does not have emergency services, it's a good idea to locate your nearest emergency vet clinic and keep their contact information on hand, just in case something happens to your precious Boxer.

Photo Courtesy of Danny Leonard

Genetic Health of Boxers

There are a few common genetic illnesses found in Boxers that you will want to keep an eye out for. Most Boxers will not develop these illnesses or injuries during their life, but it's still a good idea to be aware that these conditions are more common in this breed than in others.

Boxers are somewhat susceptible to heart disease. Cardiomyopathy and aortic stenosis are two diseases often found in this breed. Cardiomyopathy is the degeneration of the heart muscle that can lead to congestive heart failure. A dog may not be symptomatic in early stages of the disease, but will eventually show weakness, difficulty breathing, coughing, or abdominal distention. Aortic stenosis is a genetic condition where the dog is born with an aorta that is too narrow where oxygenated blood leaves the heart. Symptoms include an abnormal heart rhythm or lung sounds, difficult breathing, lethargy, and an aversion to physical activity. These are conditions that your vet may be able to diagnose at a regular appointment, but if your typically peppy Boxer is suddenly lethargic and out of breath, you should schedule a vet visit.

Bloat is another disease that is common in many dog breeds, especially breeds with a deep chest. This condition occurs when the stomach fills up with air, eventually leading to stomach torsion and a loss of blood flow. This illness can come on quickly, especially when a dog eats too quickly or exercises too vigorously after a meal. Symptoms include excessive drooling, pacing, retching without vomiting, and pain. If you suspect your dog is suffering from bloat, take him to the vet immediately, because surgery is required. This disease can be fatal if not treated urgently. To prevent bloat, buy your Boxer a dish with obstacles that make it hard to gulp food down, or impose a brief rest period between meals and playtime.

Your Boxer may also be at risk for allergies, skin irritations, and different forms of cancer. If your dog is itchy, scabby, or appears generally uncomfortable, talk to your vet about hydrocortisone lotions or even an oral antihistamine. You may also need to change your dog's diet if the dog food formula is the culprit. Cancers can be difficult to detect in dogs, but it's a good idea to feel your dog for any unusual lumps or bumps on a regular basis and see your vet if you find anything concerning. Because your vet only examines your dog on a yearly basis, the owner is the best person to notice chances in health or appearance. If these problems are caught early enough, surgery and medication may extend your dog's years.

Illness and Injury Prevention

HELPFUL TIP
Health Problems

Unfortunately, Boxers are prone to a variety of health problems including heart disease and cancer. Some of the illnesses that are more likely to affect boxers include:
- Cardiomyopathy
- Aortic/subaortic stenosis (AS/SAS)
- Degenerative myelopathy
- Gastric torsion (bloat)
- Skin problems
- Allergies
- Mast cell tumors
- Hemangiosarcoma
- Lymphoma

Boxers are active dogs who like to play hard. Sometimes, that leads to illness and injury. While you can't protect your dog from every ailment, there are a few things you can do to keep them safe and prevent issues later in life.

When it comes to food, Boxers will eat anything that comes their way. Keep any edible objects away from your dog, or else you may be dealing with a sick Boxer. Give your dog his daily meals, then put away anything he doesn't eat in one feeding. That way, he won't be grazing all day. Keep all human food in closed cupboards and pantries, especially while you're out of the house. Make sure garbage cans are inaccessible. A bored Boxer may choose to entertain himself by snacking on your meals. Not only can people food lead to weight gain, but it can make your dog ill.

Photo Courtesy of Brynn Holic

While your Boxer may like to run and jump as a young dog, some movements can cause injury to a Boxer, especially as he ages. For example, a dog may be able to jump up and down furniture without incident, but a dog with joint problems could dislocate a joint if he lands funny. Over time, the stress on joints can aggravate conditions like arthritis, making it difficult for your senior dog to get around. It is best to teach your dog not to jump on your taller furniture, but if you like having your dog on your bed, consider adding a set of steps to the foot of your bed to prevent future skeletal injuries caused by repetitive wear on joints.

Boxers are very susceptible to temperature-related illnesses. A Boxer can overheat quickly in warm weather, especially if he is active. A first-time Boxer owner may forget that this breed has a tougher time regulating body temperature, compared to other breeds. When it is warm outside, place cool water in a shady spot for your dog to relax during play. If it's hot enough that you're sweating, keep physical activity to a moderate level, or stay close to home if you're taking your dog on a walk. If you live somewhere with very cold winters, consider buying your dog boots and a jacket for walks on frigid days. When in doubt, find ways to play inside with your Boxer. A game of hide and seek in your home or a trip to the indoor dog park will help keep your dog comfortable and safe.

Caring For Your Aging Boxer

Once your Boxer is around seven or eight years old, he will be considered a senior dog. However, this doesn't mean that he's anywhere near to the end of his days! Senior dogs can continue to live a long and healthy life, but will need extra care once they begin aging.

One change you might notice if your dog's change in metabolism. Older dogs do not need as many calories as younger dogs because of their body's changes and a gradual reduction in normal activity. Therefore, many vets recommend owners switch to a senior dog food formula. This will give them the nutrients they need without giving them too many calories. If you notice your senior dog gaining weight, gradually reduce daily meals and continue gentle exercise to see if the pounds come off. If not, talk to your vet about switching to a formula that keeps senior dogs from gaining too much extra fat.

Because his body is beginning to wear down from a lifetime of play, your older Boxer may be slower and stiffer than he was as a young dog. Joint supplements may help with pain, along with any prescription anti-inflammatory meds your vet may prescribe. Be careful not to play too roughly with an old dog, nor encourage him to sprint around like he did as a pup.

Photo Courtesy of Barbra Babler

Keep daily walks short and avoid long games of fetch that require sprinting and jumping. Arthritis is common in senior dogs and can cause a lot of pain and discomfort. If your Boxer is a swimmer, he may enjoy paddling around a lake or pool for exercise. That way, he keeps some weight off of his sensitive joints.

While you may reduce your dog's physical exercise, it is still very important to keep your senior dog physically and mentally stimulated. Especially with seniors, dogs need entertainment to keep themselves from getting grouchy or depressed. Dogs can even suffer from dementia if they do not receive mental stimulation in their old age. Playtime is still a necessity, but at a less intense level. Puzzle toys filled with tasty treats can keep a senior dog entertained for a long time. Especially if your old dog's teeth are sore and chewing on boys is no longer possible, your Boxer will enjoy gently pushing levers on a puzzle board or licking peanut butter out of a rubber toy. Gentle games of fetch or catch will keep your dog happy, but make sure your senior dog doesn't have to work too hard to have fun.

Senior dogs may lose some of the puppy fat that protects their bones and joints as they age, making them uncomfortable when they rest on the hard floor. If your dog's bed is worn out, you may want to find a thicker bed to get your dog up and off of the ground. Also, if your Boxer frequently sits on the couch or lies on the bed with you, some steps or a small platform may make it easier for him to cuddle with you. Slippery floors may also pose a problem for older dogs with limited mobility, so an area rug over a hard floor can make your dog much more comfortable getting around your home.

Your Boxer may also experience blindness and deafness as he reaches old age, but this should not affect his quality of life too much. Often times, dogs progressively lose their vision as they age, but don't show it. Sometimes, dog owners don't realize their dogs are blind until they move their furniture and their dog bumps into a couch that was in their usual path.

Dogs are good at adapting to their vision loss and can get around well as long as their routines and usual paths are not changed. Hearing loss can change the way you interact with your Boxer, but it will not hurt his overall quality of life. It can be frustrating to call for your dog or give commands and have him ignore you, but understand that he will still read your nonverbal cues. If you taught your dog visual commands to accompany your verbal commands, he will understand what you want him to do, even though it is more difficult to get his attention. If your aging Boxer has both hearing and vision loss, be patient with him. He will likely respond to physical cues, like light pressure on his bottom when you need him to sit. However, don't expect too much from your elderly Boxer—at his advanced age, he will mostly want to spend time close to you and won't cause too much trouble.

When it's Time to Say Goodbye

At a certain point in a dog's life, he will likely show a steep decline in overall health. When this day comes, the owner is faced with a tough decision. No one wants to say goodbye to their best friend, but sometimes, euthanasia is the kindest option for the end of your dog's life. There are a few major signs that a dog may be too uncomfortable to continue living. A dog that is completely incontinent not only makes life difficult for the people in your household, but suggests that your dog's mental and physical health is in decline. Another sign is if your dog is unable to move, or is in obvious pain when he tries to move. A dog that cannot get up to eat or go to the bathroom will eventually face more medical issues do to a lack of nutrition and hygiene.

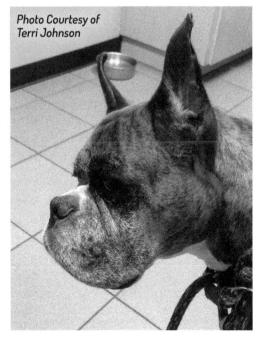

Photo Courtesy of Terri Johnson

While some medical conditions that occur in old age, like blindness, are not serious enough to warrant euthanasia, others, like cancer or incontinence, may be a sign that your dog is in too much pain to continue living. Of course, you may choose to treat cancer if the

Photo Courtesy of Rachel Walters

vet believes surgery or medication can extend your dog's years, but in some cases, surgery is too risky and medication can make a dog feel weaker. Similarly, incontinence can be dealt with by buying potty pads and diapers and frequently cleaning your dog and your home, but it can be a symptom of a larger issue. Your Boxer may be suffering from mobility issues or painful urinary tract infections that don't seem to go away. Many owners will do what they can to prolong their dog's life, but advanced age and ill health can make it difficult to see positive results.

If a dog reaches this stage in his life, it's best to see the vet to find a solution to the symptoms before requesting euthanasia. Sometimes, a dog appears to be on his last leg, but a new medication extends his quality of life for another year. Your vet is also has a lot of experience in this department and can help you make an end of life decision. However, understand that a vet cannot make the choice for you. You can ask for advice, but ultimately, you must make the call.

When the day comes, you will have the choice to stay in the room or leave. While it can be extremely hard to see a pet go, your Boxer will be comforted by your presence during the painless procedure. This is something no owner wants to prepare for, but it's important to know your options when the day comes. The dog will get an injection of a very powerful sedative and will drift off to sleep. The drug will cause the dog's heart to stop beating within the minute. A euthanized animal will not feel any pain during this quick process. Apart from the potential of fear from being at the vet and the quick pinch of the needle, this process is not painful or scary to a dog. If anything, a dog in pain may feel relief before he drifts off.

The time after a pet's death can be difficult for the owner. For those who are sentimental about their pets, vet clinics are willing to return the cremains to the owner and will likely have different options for urns to purchase. Laws about burying pets vary from location to location, so check your local laws or ask a vet before going in that direction. Otherwise, there are other ways to memorialize your beloved Boxer. Keep pictures around your home to remind you of the happy times with your dog. Donate to an animal shelter or Boxer rescue in memory of your dog. If you're not ready for a new pet but miss spending time around dogs, volunteer at a shelter or help a neighbor by walking their dogs. If the grieving process is difficult, one of the best things you can do is give back and help other dogs. Then, when you're ready, take some time to find your next best friend. Of course, a new dog will never replace your beloved Boxer in your heart, but that doesn't mean that you should never find a new dog to love.